SICILY

Art, history and natural beauty

EDITION

OGB officina
grafica
bolognese SRL

info@ogbsrl.it
Distributor: Parisi Antonio
Mobile: +39 338 7661856

Geographical Information

Sicily, in every respect, is the largest island in the Mediterranean Sea, measuring 25,738 sq.Km. Situated in the middle of the Mediterranean, its triangular shape earned it the name "Trinacria", which in ancient Greek means "land of three promontories"; Peloro Point to the north-east, Cape Lilibeo to the west and Cape Correnti to the south-east. However, it has been argued that the name "Trinacria" derives from the word "Trinacia" the famous city of the "Siculi" (inhabitants of Sicily in this period) destroyed by the Syracusans in 493 a.C.

Its triangular form is highlighted in its orographical detail which shows the three corners of the island as the extreme points of three mountainous chains emanating from a central knot. On one side the mountainous relief is a continuation of the Apennine Mountains and on the other side a continuation of the mountainous area of the Tunisian Atlantic. Sicily is, for the most part a land of hills and mountains with very few lowland areas. On the east coast we can see the chain of mountains known as the Peloritani which run from Messina to Novara di Sicilia with the characteristic "fiumare" small streams that flow on vast pebbly river beds. The Nebrodi Mountains run from this point as far as Gangi under the name of Caronie and continue until they join the Madonie Mountain Range which includes II Pizzo Della Principessa (The Princess's Lace) at 1,975 metres, the second highest mountain peak after Mount Etna. To the south the sulphurous tableland from which sulphur for industrial purposes is mined, dominates the area. To the east the plateau known as the Erei Mountains can be distinguished by its sulphurous, chalk base covered by a layer of volcanic tufa rock which allows a certain amount of vegetation to flourish. On this tufa crust the cities of Enna and Piazza Armerina are founded. To the south-east the Hyablaen Mountains rise. They are made of marine-lava and whitish limestone on which four famous cities, Ragusa, Modica, Noto and Syracuse were built. The most famous volcano on the island, Mount Etna dominates the east coast from a height of 3,500 metres. However, there are other volcanoes on the Aeolian Islands including active ones like those of Vulcano, Stromboli, Ustica and Pantelleria. To the south of Mount Etna the once marshy plain of Catania is now rich, arable land where orangeries and vineyards are cultivated. There are many other vineyards famous for the production of fine wines in Trapani, Marsala, Mazara del Vallo and Castelvetrano. The group of smaller islands is completed by the Egadi Isles. The whole of Sicily is well-known for its mild climate and clear skies. Rain falls mainly in winter and summers are dry. Changeable winds blow over the island for most of the year but in summer tropical air currents prevail. The driest month of the year is July while the wettest is November. The climate is characteristically maritime with summers that do not exceed those of Northern Italy in temperature but which have the advantage of much milder winters.

The first inhabitants of Sicily were the "Sicani" and later the "Siculi" who, according to Paolo Orsi were originally Lybian-Hispanic tribes from Africa. The former were the forefathers of the latter and this is evident from their names which indicate different, progressive stages of the same race. The "Sican" Civilization developed in the Neolithic Age in which the legends of the Cyclops and the Lystrogons have their roots. The few Paleolithic remains found on the island also belong to this civilization. The eneolithical "Siculi" left behind burial chambers scattered all over the island together with remnants of pottery which are now stored in museums in Palermo and Syracuse. Despite the influx of foreigners to the island, these two races form one unique civilization which evolved in the 2nd Millennium and continued to develop up until the beginning of the 5th century B.C. The Egeo-Mycenians traded with the "Seculi" distributing their goods among them and paving the way for the Greek colonies which were to follow. In the 8th and 7th centuries B.C. the Greeks began to expand their colonies intensely and both Doric and Calcidic peoples settled in Sicily. The cities of Naxos (735 B.C.), Syracuse (734 B.C.), Leontinoi (Lentini), Kàtane (Catania), Megara, Hyblea, Zacle (Messina), Gela, Megara and Syracuse were founded and flourished to such an extent that other colonies were established under the government of Doric Syracuse and managed to gather together all the Hellenic forces against two common enemies. These were the "Siculi" who refused to tolerate a nation of people that they considered to be foreigners and the Cartheginians who were threatening the island from the east. The salvation of the Hellenic civilization was due in part to Akragas' mother at Gela from which the Dinomenidi family derives. Two great monarchs came from this family, Hippocrates, conqueror of the "Siculi" at Hibla Herea (492 B.C.) and the other, Gelone, the Syracusan tyrant who, as head of the Syracusan and Akragant armies defeated the Carthaginians at Imera in 480 B.C. saving the island from the barbaric Punic invaders. From this historic moment the history of Hellenistic Sicily overlaps with that of the city of Syracuse, which not only consolidated but extended its influence under Ierone I, the conqueror of the Etruscans at Enna in 474 B.C. The success of Syracusan dominance excited the jealousy of Athens which tried to reassert itself in a battle which ended in the defeat of the Athenian fleet at the port of Syracuse. The ensuing threat by the Cartheginians was quelled by the action of a valiant and energetic man named Dionigi "il Vecchio" (The Old) who managed to suppress civil strife among his people, uniting both "Siculi" and Greeks against the barbarians. Timoleonte of Corinth, another great historical figure, reinforced this unity in the face of a renewed threat posed by the Cartheginians, however the slow process of decline which had already set in was too much even for Agatocle to tackle. Agatocle, another important figure in Sicilian history, was a tyrant of Syracuse who led his army against the Cartheginians in Africa. The king of the Epiri, Piro, was called by the Greeks to take back the island from the Cartheginians. The mercenary army of the Mamertini succeeded in taking Messina and began looting and plundering the surrounding towns, Ierone II was on the point of beating them back with the help of his Carthaginian allies when the Mamertini asked Rome for protection against him. Rome intervened and the beginning of the Punic Wars was sealed with the main aim of conquering the whole island for Rome itself. After numerous events such as the "Ten year Seige of Lilibeo" by the Romans, the revolt led by Amilcare Barca on Mount Pellegrino (Pil-

grim Mountain), the seige of Mount Erice and the final terrible defeat of the Cartheginians in the Egadi Sea in 241, Rome finally gained control over Sicily. The island became Rome's granary but unfortunately unscrupulous speculators created large land estates for themselves which were worked by slaves and as time went on the region became poorer and poorer. The town of Verre was plundered and Sesto Pompeo took advantage of the island's wealth. Another Roman Emperor Augustus tried in vane to improve conditions on the island which then fell prey to the Vandals and the Ostrogoths. In 535 Belisario freed the island from these invaders and annexed it to the Eastern Empire. The island's decline lasted for more than three centuries, however when the Byzantines decided to transfer their capital city from Constantinople to Syracuse in 663 under Eraclio Costante the island was given a new lease of life. In the 6th century, slowly but surely the Arabs began to infiltrate into Sicily, taking advantage of the general state of abandon that they found there and in 831 they conquered Palermo. They went on to conquer Enna in 858, Syracuse in 878 and the Fortress of Taormina in 901. Two dynasties, the Aglabite and the Fatimis governed Saracen Sicily bringing back prosperity to the island. The capital city became Palermo and was the seat of the Emiro. In 1038 the island was conquered by Maniace for the Emperor Michele Paflagonio and in 1060 Count Ruggero of Altavilla conquered Messina, then Palermo, Syracuse, Girgenti, Castrogiovanni and Butera with only a hand full of Norman knights. Roberto Gius-

cardo, assuming the title Duke of Sicily and Ruggero assuming the title Count of Sicily divided the island between them, however, when Ruggero died in 1101 there were no more male descendants of Roberto to succeed him, so Ruggero's son, Simone acceded to the throne followed by his younger brother Ruggero II aided by his mother Adelasia. Ruggero inherited the dukedom of Puglia and was crowned in Palermo Cathedral on Christmas Day 1130. He was a successful soldier winning many battles and extended his domain as far as Corinth, Athens and Thebes. At his magnificent court both Arab and Christian cultures were united. When he died in 1154 his son Guglielmo, nick-named "Il Malo" (The Bad) succeeded him. However, it was his other son Guglielmo II "Il Buono" (The Good) who founded the Cathedral of Monreale and governed well until 1189, when he died at the age of 36. His daughter Costanza, became the wife of Arrigo di Swabia who was Federico Barbarossa's son. Ruggero's only direct male descendent was his illegitimate son, Prince Tancredi, a man of great intellect who was proclaimed king of Sicily in 1190. When Tancredi died in 1194, the crown went to his young son Guglielmo under the guidance of his mother. In the meantime, Arrigo had arrived in Sicily claiming the crown for himself. He had the young prince blinded and imprisoned also incarcerating Tancredi's widow and daughters. He earned himself the title of "crudele" (the cruel) for his harsh treatment of the barons whom he had tortured and killed. His son, Federico II born in Italy succeeded him after his death in 1197. Federico proved to be a great monarch and a follower of modern thinking. He established a splendid court at his palace in Palermo and was a great patron of the arts, literature and science. After his death in 1250, his son Corrado succeeded him but after only four years on the throne the crown was passed down to his younger brother, Corradino, who was still a child. The valiant Manfredi, Corrado's half-brother claimed the throne going against the wishes of the Pope who wanted Charles of Anjou, King Louis IX of France's brother to conquer the south of Italy and the island of Sicily. The victory at the Battle of Benevento and Manfredi's death in combat secured the realm for Charles of Anjou. Two years later he defeated Corradino at Tagliacozzo and had the young king beheaded in Naples. Rebellious French noblemen provoked the Sicilian Vesper in 1282 and Charles of Anjou attempted in vain to win back the rebellious island. Pietro d'Aragona, Manfredi's daughter's husband was summoned to take charge of Sicily and with his government the new Dynasty of Aragon was born. Unfortunately it was not very successful in controlling the all-powerful feudal lords. The chronicles from this period are full of descriptions of the violent confrontations that took place between arrogant lords and the governing authorities. The island lost its independence under the rule of Martino II, however his reign also brought an end to the confusion over who had a right to claim the throne. After the death of Martino the Dynasty of Castigle began which did nothing but worsen the country's troubles even under the wise guidance of Prince Alfonso il Magnanimo (so called The Magnanimous). From the 1400s onwards Sicily's history takes the form of a succession of viceroys, often incapable and greedy for money. This situation often erupted into violent rebellions in which much blood was shed (in Palermo the Revolt of F. Squarcialupo 1517, the Rebellion of G. D'Alesi 1647 and in Messina the Revolution of 1674-78). In 1713, the Utrecht Peace Treaty which brought about the end of the War of Spanish Succession was signed and Sicily was given to Vittorio Amedeo of Savoy solemnly crowned in Palermo. Unfortunately, he was then forced to exchange Sicily for Sardinia with the Spanish King Philip V. The reign of the two Sicilies began under Philip V of Bourbon and continued under the rule of Charles III, an enlightened and reformistic sovereign bringing an improvement to the condition of Naples and Sicily. However, after the succession of the young Spanish monarch to the throne Sicily, once more began to decline. Although Sicily endured the ineptitudes of incapable monarchs like Federico I (nick-named "nasone" or "Big Nose") it did not rebel even against the religious and aristocratic despots during the French Revolution. In 1812 the Sicilian Parliament abolished feudalism which had plagued the country for ages. The Carboneria Intrigue, the motions of 1920 and 21 which gave way to a demand for a written constitution for which permission was first granted and then denied (1812-15), the cholera epidemic in 1837 and the ferocious repression carried out by the state pushed the Sicilian people to the limits. On January 12th 1848 the population rose unanimously to rid the country of its tyrants. A provisional government was formed under Ruggero Settimo and the Sicilian Parliament declared that the Bourbon Dynasty had officially come to an end. The crown was offered to and refused by Alberto Amedeo of Savoy. The island once again abandoned to itself could not resist against attacks by the Neapolitan military forces commanded by Filangeri. Messina, Catania, Syracuse, Palermo and some minor cities capitulated and while the ferocious restoration movement raged in 1849 the Sicilians waited hopefully for their liberation which came on 4th April 1860 to the sound of the bells of the Gangia Convent in Palermo. The insurrection instigated by Francesco Riso ended in bloodshed; these were to be the last 13 victims whose lives were lost because of civil upheaval. Garibaldi arrived with his "Mille da Quarto" (One Thousand) army on 5th May. He landed at Marsala on 11th and was heralded as a liberator. In a few weeks he had regained the whole island. We only need to record the most important dates of this historical event which were 14th May the proclamation of Salemi, 15th May the victory of Calatafimi, 27th May Palermo was taken, 17th July victory of Milazzo and 27th July Messina was taken. The Sicilian language bears witness to its long and turbulent history. The Greek influence is more evident in its Byzantine "Greekness" rather than in its Magna "Greekness" in its pure form. There are many traces of Germanic and English expressions in the language and Arab domination has also left its mark, especially in the place names. Even the Normans and Anjovin domination have deposited a considerable number of words in Sicilian vocabulary.

Crossing the Messina Straits which separate the Italian mainland from the Island of Sicily you can see the modern city of Messina rising between the sea and the hills and in the background you can make out the Peloritan Mountains. A long the Straits you can still see the places that Homer wrote about (Scilla and Carybdis) the terrifying whirlpools and strong currents which are caused by a difference in the level between the Tyrrhenian Sea and the Ionian Sea. The ancient city of Zancle (sythe) so called because of the sythe-shaped piece of land which closes the mouth of the port, was once a Greek colony and was then inhabited by the Myseni who gave the city its name of Messana. The city was influenced by both Byzantine and Norman civilisations and was a great humanistic centre in Medieval times. In 1600 it was repressed after an abortive rebellion against Spanish rule. In the 18th century a series of disasters overwhelmed the island; the plague, earthquakes and invasions by Barbarians took their toll on the population of Messina. In 1854 there was a cholera epidemic and on December 28th 1908 the city was completely destroyed by an earthquake which caused great waves to flood the land. As a result the whole city was rebuilt. Houses were constructed to be earthquake-proof and roads were made straight and wide. The city was also the target of air-raids during the last World War and it is because of these that the city now has such a modern appearance and has become a large commercial and tourist centre. Among the famous inhabitants of Messina were the philosopher Dicearcus (4th cent. B.C.) and Aristocles (2nd cent. B.C.), the poet Guido and Oddo delle Colonne (13th cent.), the painter Antonello da Messina (15th cent.) and the historian/politician Giuseppe La Farina (1815 - 1863). **The Cathedral** was almost entirely rebuilt in recent times, The only remaining original part of the façade is the lower half with its marquetry in relief depicting ethnological and historical subjects. The precious Gothic porticos are of the 16th century and the central arch is between two stylized lions which sustain valuable columns overhung by reliefs and statues. The church spire is of particular interest because of its un-

The Cathedral

Detail of the church tower

usual astronomical clock which was built by Teodoro Ungerer of Strasbourg and inaugurated by the Bishop of Paino and is the largest in the world. When this clock strikes mid-day various clockwork figures begin to move. Two heroines from the history of Messina (Dina and Clarenza) a lion that roars, a cockerel that opens its wings and crows, the Madonna of the Letters, protector of the city and the Sanctuary of Montalto. Inside, the Cathedral has a wooden ceiling dating from Medieval times. Many works of art have been substituted by copies of the originals like the pulpit, the baldacchino, the mosaic on the main alter, the statues and the baptistery. There is a great master-piece entitled "The Baptist" by Gagini which can be admired at the first alter on the right.

There is also a very interesting exhibition of "Treasures" made up of goblets from the 14th - 17th centuries, relics from the 12th - 17th centuries, chandeliers and valuable embroidery in gold and silver thread from the 17th century, chasubles and copes made of silk, rings, seals, precious sceptres, sculpted corals, silverware from 17th and 18th centuries and Byzantine paintings. The gold "manta" and the silver "vascelluzzo" are of great interest. In front of the Cathedral you can see the **Orione Fountain** in the large square, it is the work of G.A.Montorsoli (16th century). The fountain represents the mythical founder of the city depicted on two cups held up by mythological figures that are stuck to a many-sided bath decorated with allegorical sculptures of the Tiber, the Nile, the Ebro and the Camaro.

The Orione Fountain

Panorama

The beautiful Norman church of **St. Annunziata of the Catalans** overlooks a small square not far from the Cathedral. It was built in the 12th century and some of its original stone work can still be seen; for example the transept, the cupola and the apse. Inside there is a nave with two aisles. The central nave shows barrel vaults while those on either side show cross vaulting.

The Regional Museum is situated near St. Margherita Hospital and has many archaeological and prehistoric exhibits on display. It also has a collection of paintings, ceramics, sculptures and artefacts made of gold and silk, which are of interest. There is a polyptych of S. Gregorio di Antonello da Messina (1473) and two paintings by Caravaggio, The Adoration of the Shepherds and The Resurrection of Lazarus which can be seen in the picture gallery. Also in the picture gallery, you can see various sculptures like the *Madonna degli Storpi* by Goro di Gregorio (14th cent.), the statue of Saint

The Church of Ss. Annunziata dei Catalani

Anthony of Padua by Antonello Gagini and the famous Scilla (Scylla) by Montosoli. To get to Villa Mazzini where the Municipal Aquarium is housed you leave via Garibaldi and walk around the harbour. There is also a museum of marine life in the same building. **The Fortress of Saint Salvatore** stands on the furthermost point of the port. It was built in the 16th century by the Spanish and has a column surmounted by a statue of the Virgin Mary in the act of benediction.

The Fountain of Neptune embellishes the Piazza dell'Unità d'Italia and is the work of Montorsoli (1557). The god of the sea, Neptune is depicted pacifying the waves and at his side you can see two mermaids, Scylla and Carybdis. These three statues are copies of the originals which are housed in the city museum for reasons of preservation.

The Neptune Fountain

The Polyptych showing The Virgin Mary and Child

This city is one of the most important in the Messina area. It is situated at the end of a long, narrow peninsula which forms a natural port with numerous sandy beaches. From here you can get to the *Aeolian Islands*. The oldest part of the city is higher up than the modern part and in it you can see the medieval castle begun by Frederick II of Swabia and completed in the 16th century by the Arabs. The castle has an irregular form and is surrounded by strong walls interspersed with huge semicircular towers. Note the magnificent 14th century portal. As the castle was used for a considerable period of time as a prison it has undergone many structural changes over the years. Tombs dating back to the Greek and "Seculi" civilizations have been excavated in the area

The harbour

surrounding the castle. The New Cathedral can be seen in the newer part of the city and houses valuable paintings from the 15th and 16th centuries; for example The Adoration of Baby Jesus, St. Thomas Aquinus, St. Paul, St. Peter and St. Rocco, by Antonello de Saliba and also the Annunciation and St. Nicholas painted by Antonio Giuffrè.

The Church of Saint Salvatore

The Castello Luna

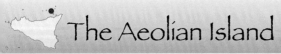

The Aeolian Island

Seven islands make up the archipelago in the Tyrrhenian Sea just north of Milazzo, called the Aeolians and they are Lipari, Vulcano, Salina, Panarea, Stromboli, Filicudi, and Alicudi.

There are regular ferries that run from Milazzo and you can also sail to the Aeolians from Messina, Palermo, Cefalù, Reggio Calabria and Naples. The islands are made of volcanic rock with steep craggy coastlines. The town of Stromboli and Vulcano still have active volcanoes and you can see geysers and hot-water springs at Lipari and Panarea. The main economy of these islands apart from tourism is fishing and agriculture. Lipari is famous for its Malvasia wine, its olives, almonds and capers. From here the famous pumice stone is exported all over the world. The first inhabitants of these islands date back to the Neolithic Period (4th Millennium B.C.) who used the obsidian which here they found in abundance, to make sharp spear heads and blades. Obsidian is a kind of volcanic glass which is very hard wearing. It came out of the volcanic

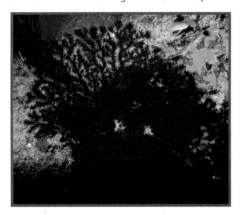

crater on the island of Lipari. Later the islands became Greek colonies in 575 B.C. and were allied with Syracuse against the Cartheginians. In 252 B.C. the islands came under Roman rule and were used as holiday resorts and naval bases. In 1544 a Turkish fleet of 144 ships landed at Lipari besieging and ruthlessly plundering the town. From this date onwards Lipari has always been considered as a refuge for Tunisian pirates.

Panorama

Lipari is the largest of the seven islands measuring 37,6 sq.Km. It is 9,5 km. long and 5 km. wide. The coasts are steep and craggy with high cliff faces. Mount Chirica is 602 m. high. A castle built by the Spanish in the 16th century can be seen with its thick surrounding walls. There is also a church of Norman origin which was reconstructed in the 13th century and renovated in 1654. It has a 19th century façade and a baroque interior. A silver statue of Saint Bartholomew from the 18th century sits on the alter. The Aeolian Archaeological Museum is situated in the grounds of the church and is divided into different sections.

Archaeological excavations

Lipari

Vulcano is the southernmost island measuring 21 sq. km. Legend has it that this was where Aeolo, the mythical god of the winds lived.

Therapeutic mud-baths on Vulcano Island

Salina is shaped like a trapezoid and has two volcanic masses which are the Porri mountain and the Fern Ditch Mountain. It is the greenest island in the whole of the archipelago. Its hills are covered with vineyards where the grapes used to make *Malvasia wine* are grown.

Panarea is the smallest of all the islands measuring only 3.4 sq. km. It is surrounded by sheer cliff faces and dominated by the huge Timpone del Corvo Volcano which is 421 m. high.

Stromboli is a four-sided box-shape with an area of 12.6 sq. km. There is only one active volcanic vent. The eastern side of the island is rich in vegetation but the central area, by contrast is barren and arid.

Strombolicchio

Filicudi is a rather isolated steep cone shape measuring 9.5 sq. km. Its highest point is Fossa Felci (Fern Ditch) which reaches 774 m. in height. The island was once called Phoenicusa because it was covered by ferns.

Alicudi forms an almost perfect circle measuring 5.2 sq. km. It was once called Ericusa, because of the abundance of heather (Erica, as it is called in Italian) which grows on the island.

The city of Tindari is built on the promontory which bears the same name. It was originally founded by Dioneges II in 396 B.C. under the name of Tyndaris.

Excavations of ancient Tyndaris show straight, parallel roads lined with houses and shops and with a sewer running under the streets of the town.

Among the finds brought to light by archaeological excavations is a *Greek Theatre*, a *Basilica* and the *thermal baths* dating back to the 2nd century B.C. The baths are decorated with marvellous mosaics as are the frigidarium (cold bath) and the caldarium (hot bath) with its underground heating system that circulated hot air under the floor and which can still be seen.

The remains of a beautiful Roman villa from the 1st century B.C. can be seen in the vicinity. The peristyle is surrounded by eight columns on each of its four sides. The great banqueting hall has beautifully painted walls and floors of wedged marble.

The ancient city still maintains in tact, its five towers and in the local *museum* you can find archaeological remains and works of art from the Greek and Roman periods. From the top of *Mount Belvedere* you can enjoy breath-taking views of the bay below and of the Aeolian Islands.

The more recent **Santuario** (Sanctuary) overlooks the square and is a holy destination of pilgrimage. It is thought that the higher part of the sanctuary was an ancient acropolis which lies near the 16th century sanctuary. Inside you can see the famous Madonna Nera (Black Madonna) which dates back to the Byzantine period and reflects eastern influences in its style.

Panorama

A view of the lakes

The Greek Theatre

The ruins of the Roman villa

The black Madonna

Sanctuary

This enchanting city overlooking the Tyrrhenian Sea is built upon a promontory which is overshadowed by a huge rocky crag shaped like a human head. in fact the word "Kefalè" means "head" in Greek.

Its origins are unknown but it was the hub of Greek, Roman, Byzantine and Arab life. Ruggero II had many architectural improvements carried out. The Cathedral was built as a means of releasing himself from a religious vow that he had taken during a storm at sea. It also served as a Pantheon for his family. The residential area of the town is a hexagonal shape divided into two parts separated by the Ruggero Road. The east side of the Corso nearest the cliff face shows the characteristic transversal roads and steps so typical of Mediaeval urban plans, while the west side nearest to the sea is made up of linear blocks of modern buildings.

The monumental centre of the city is the Cathedral Square where the Sanctuary dating from the 16th century, the Bishop's Palace dating from 1793, the Town Hall housed in the old St. Catherine's Monastery (14th century), the Palazzo Piriaino and the Palazzo Maria where Ruggero II resided, are sights that must be seen.

The Marina

Panorama

The Cathedral

The Cathedral

The Cathedral manifests the archetypal Norman religious structure and is, for this reason, very similar to the Monreale Cathedral. Work on the Cathedral which was begun in the first half of the 12th cent.were left unfinished. There is a staircase decorated with statues giving access to the churchyard. There are also two impressive towers balanced out by two smaller towers with mullioned windows with two lights and also windows with one light only, which frame the façade of the building. The façade is decorated by blind arches and woven arches with a distinctive Islamic flavour. The lower portico dates back to the 15th cent.and is attributed to Ambrogio da Como. The interior design is similar to that of the Basilica with its two aisles and central nave, thick columns artistically decorated capitals in Roman and Corinthian style, which support arches that reflect Arab influence. One of the Madonnas of Gagini from the 16th century is on display in the left nave and to the right of it there is an interesting 12th century baptismal font. The entrance to the transept is through a pointed arch supported by stout columns on either side. The floor is decorated with mosaics and on it you can see the royal throne and the Episcopal throne decorated with marquetry. In the absidal alcove you can see the Cristo Pantocrate on a gold background in the act of benediction, surrounded by the Virgin Mary, the apostles and the archangels.

Cristo
Pantocratore

The Mandralisca Museum houses numerous valuable paintings from the 15th to the 18th century among which there is the magnificent oil painting by Antonello da Messina entitled "Ritratto di Ignoto" (Portrait of an Unknown) from 1470. There are also fragments of an ancient Roman pavement, Byzantine icons and other objects of archaeological interest such as the bowl from Lipari showing an effigy of a tunny-fish monger (4th century B.C.). The remains of a megalithic construction called **The Temple of Diana** can still be seen dating from the 4th - 3rd centuries standing on the hill top.

A winding road leads to the Sanctuary di Gibilmanna where there is a valuable alter and a statue of the Madonna by Gagini.

Portrait of the unknown

The medieval Wash-house

The lighthouse

Imera ~ Solunto

Imera. The most westerly of the Greek colonies, Imera lies on the north coast of Sicily. It was founded by colonies from Zancle (Messina) in 648 B.C. and was the homeland of the famous Greek poet Stesichorus.

In 480 A.C. Gelone of Syracuse and Terone of Agrigento inflicted a decisive defeat on the Chartheginians led by Hannibal. In 409 B.C. Hannibal, Hamilcar's nephew destroyed the city. The remains of a Doric temple can still be seen near the left bank of the central river Imera. It was a hexastyle temple with six columns at the front and fourteen a long the sides and a long a base with steps leading up to it. It is thought that this site might be where the battle took place in 480 B.C. Two large lions were excavated at the same time as the temple, which are now housed in the museum in Palermo.

The Doric Temple

Solunto. There is quite allot of archaeological evidence that has been produced from the ruins of the ancient city of Solus, one of the three major Phoenician towns in the west of Sicily to demonstrate the influence of the Hellenistic and Roman periods. The street plan with its roads crossing each other at right angles, the theatre with a seating capacity for 1,200 spectators and the stage are some of the surviving buildings. Other interesting sights are the public water cistern, the remains of flooring, the square, the room thought to be a **gymnasium** because of an inscription written in Greek found here, which mentions a gym but that is in fact a two storied peristyle of a Roman villa with Doric columns above and Ionic columns on the lower tier. The house of Leda, so called because the mother of the twin gods Castor and Pollux, Leda is depicted with a swan in one of the frescoes on the wall of the house. The house is on three levels. On the first floor there were some shops, on the second a large uncovered area and the third was where the actual living quarters of the house were. From the excavation site on top of the Catalfano Mountain you can enjoy the marvellous view of the sea from Cape Zafferano to Cefalù and the mountains beyond as far as Mount Etna.

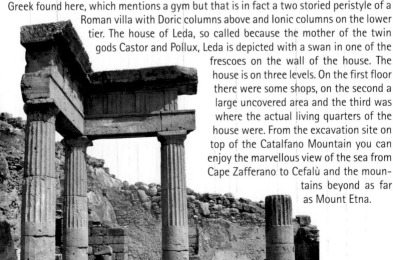

Doric columns

Monreale

Monreale is built on the slopes of the Caputo Mountain which overshadows the Conca d'Oro and the Oreto Valley. **The Cathedral** built by order of Guglielmo II in 1174, has preserved all its ancient splendour in tact. The façade has an 18th cent. colonnade of three arches surmounted by a balcony which runs between the two square towers on either side of it. The arched doorway with its shutters in bronze was designed by Bonanno Pisano in 1186 and depicts scenes from the Bible. Inside the walls are almost entirely covered with mosaics and the ceilings are covered with painted beams adding to the splendour of the interior. The floor is made of granite and porphyry. The mosaics which cover an area equivalent to 6.000 m.sq. were composed between the end of the 12th cent. and the middle of the 13th cent. and illustrate scenes from the Old and New Testaments.

In the central apse there is an effigy of

The Cathedral

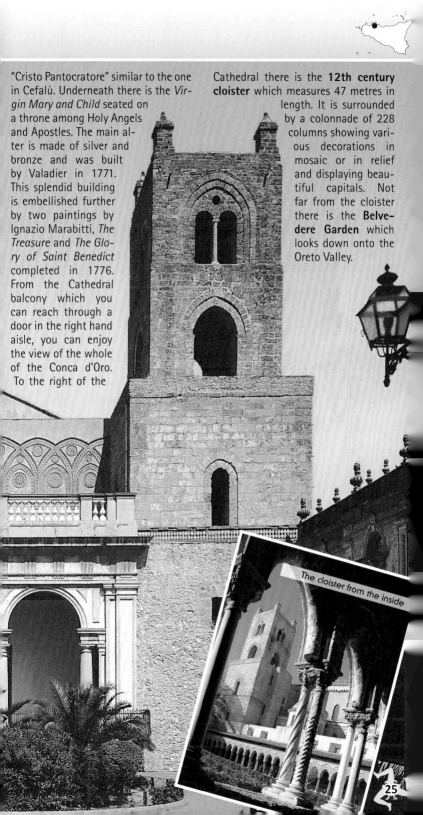

"Cristo Pantocratore" similar to the one in Cefalù. Underneath there is the *Virgin Mary and Child* seated on a throne among Holy Angels and Apostles. The main alter is made of silver and bronze and was built by Valadier in 1771. This splendid building is embellished further by two paintings by Ignazio Marabitti, *The Treasure* and *The Glory of Saint Benedict* completed in 1776. From the Cathedral balcony which you can reach through a door in the right hand aisle, you can enjoy the view of the whole of the Conca d'Oro. To the right of the Cathedral there is the **12th century cloister** which measures 47 metres in length. It is surrounded by a colonnade of 228 columns showing various decorations in mosaic or in relief and displaying beautiful capitals. Not far from the cloister there is the **Belvedere Garden** which looks down onto the Oreto Valley.

The cloister from the inside

Cristo Pantocratore

Palermo

The city of Palermo lies in a splendid position in the generous cove known as the **Conca d'Oro** dominated by Pellegrino Mountain. It is the capital city of the Autonomous Sicilian Region. It was called Ziz (flower) by the Phoenicians and Panormus (All Harbour) by the Greeks. The area has been inhabited since prehistoric times and was known as a Punic settlement and later a Roman colony. From 535 to 831 it was under Byzantine rule, and in 1072 it was seized by the Saracens who made the city thrive once more turning it into one of the most beautiful cities of that period. Ruggero II also contributed to the development of the city making it the capital after the Norman conquest. It became a hub of commercial activity and was of great artistic and cultural consequence. In fact, it is in this period that buildings such as the Cathedral, the Palatina Chapel, the Martorana, St. John of the Hermits, S. Cataldo and the Zisa and the Cuba were built. It underwent a period of decline under the Anjovins who were expelled from the city during the Revolt of the Vespri in 1282. After this date the Aragonese took possession of the city restoring it to its former prosperity. The distinctly Baroque style of the ancient city centre can be traced back to the times of Spanish dominance. The Bourbon government tried to establish a constitution in a vain attempt to stem the tide of revolution in 1812, however this was not enough to deter Garibaldi's Army of Mille in 1860.

Via Cavour to the north and Corso Tukory and Via Lincoln to the south set the boundaries of the ancient city centre which is divided into four areas by two roads

that cross each other at right angles, Via Vittorio Emanuele and Via Maqueda and meet in the beautiful Vigliena Square, commonly known as the Quattro Canti. From this square many typically Medieval roads emanate.

The city has developed and expanded over the area between the harbour and Mount Pellegrino.

Quattro Canti is also known as Vigliena Square because of the rounded corners of the buildings that meet at the crossing between Via Vittorio Emanuele and Via Maqueda and form a really Baroque setting with statues of the Spanish Kings, the Fountains of the Seasons and royal and imperial coats of arms everywhere.

S. Giuseppe dei Teatini (Saint Joseph of Teatini) in via Vittorio Emanuele was erected in 1612 and modified in the following century by the addition of the dome. The interior is divided into two aisles and a central nave which is elaborately decorated with marble, stucco-work and frescoes.

Quattro Canti

Panorama

Piazza Pretoria (Pretoria Square) is dominated by the fountain which was originally meant for the Florentine residence of Don Pietro of Toledo. However, it was purchased to decorate the piazza of the People's Senate. It was created by two Florentine artists, Francesco Cammilliani and Michelangelo Naccherini who sculpted the monstrous mythological figures of pagan gods and animals that pour water into a large ring-shaped basin and other smaller basins. The fountain which was built on steps and surrounded by railings forms a circle on two levels separated by a pool of water. In the centre there is a marble column on top of which a cherub holds a horn of plenty.

Pretoria Square

Piazza Bellini is dominated by two splendid monuments, the Martorana and S. Cataldo (Saint Cataldo). The Church of Martorana, also known as the church of S. Maria dell'Ammiraglio (The Church of Saint Mary of the Admiral). This church is of Norman construction and dates back to 1143 when Admiral Giorgio d'Antiochia, commander of Ruggero II's fleet had it built. Since then it has undergone significant overhauls especially in the 16th and 17th centuries (a Baroque façade on the left side). The four-storey bell tower is of great elegance with its tracery windows with two lights and polychrome inlays. Unfortunately, the dome was lost after it collapsed in the 1726 earthquake disaster. If you walk under the bell tower you will come to an "atrium" divided by columns built in the 17th century. In the previous construction this construction substituted the present portico which linked the church to the bell-tower. The mosaic vestments dating back to 1143 are extraordinary and it is easy to find similarities between these and Byzantine art and also evidence of a new stylistic direction such as that found in the Palatina Chapel and in the Cathedral of Cefalù. The Christ Pantocratore and the Saints Ciro and Giovanni Cristostomo are attributed to one artist while the four archangels on the dome ceiling, the eight apostles and the annunciation scene have been attributed to another. The classical, refined style suggests that the prophets and the evangelists blowing the trumpet painted on the ceiling of the dome are the work of a different artist. *The Nativity* and *The Virgin's Journey* are immersed in lyricism. The two panels depicting the coronation of Ruggero by Christ and in which the main figures lack corpulence was definitely done by another artist.

Perhaps the church that manages to preserve Arab style and culture best of all is S. Cataldo with its well-defined geometrical forms, blind arches and elegant crenelated surrounds. It was built around 1160 and has managed to preserve its interior in tact. there are no mosaic coverings here. The church is divided into two aisles and a central nave made up of six ancient columns which support arabesque arches while three small domes on corner stones surmount the central nave. Even the floor is original.

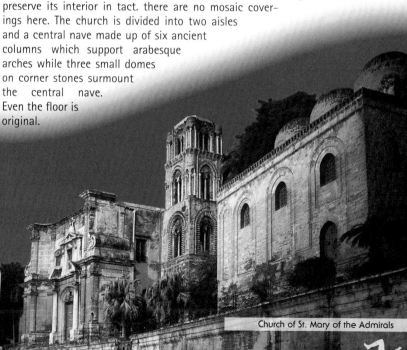

Church of St. Mary of the Admirals

Palermo

The Cathedral rises majestically on the edge of a garden surrounded by a Baroque marble wall decorated with statues and was built by order of the Archbishop Gualtiero Offanilio in 1184 on the site of a mosque. Over the years the church has undergone numerous reconstructions and improvements. In the 14th century the four bell towers were raised and between the 15th and the 16th centuries the south and central colonnades were built. The façade is typically 14th/15th century in style *and is* flanked by two ornate bell-towers decorated with sculptures that are reminiscent of Islamic art in their use of abstract designs and vegetation.

The Catalan-Gothic southern portico dating back to the second half of the 15th century overlooks the square. Inside the numerous restorations undertaken by men like F. Fuga in the 18th century are evident especially the aisles and the nave which are decorated with giant sculptures of the saints supported by pillars. In an enclosure in the right nave you can see the imperial and royal tombs of Henry VI who died in 1197, Frederick II of Swabia who died in 1250, The Empress Con-

stance, his wife who died in 1198 and of Constance's father Ruggero V who died in 1154. In the right hand part of the presbytery, lies the Chapel of Saint Rosalia where there is a silver urn containing the relics of the saint, surrounded by protective bronze railings. To the right of the apse you can reach the ante-sacrestia where a 15th century door leads to the Sala del Tesoro (Treasury) in which many church ornaments, chalices, monstrances and miniatures from the 14th and 18th centuries are carefully stored. In the new sacrestia, a Virgin Mary attributed to Gagini can be admired.

The Sacramento Chapel in the left transept guards a precious 17th century tabernacle in lapis lazzuli by a master of Bergamo. The crypt consists of two transversal naves interspersed by granite columns that hold up cross vaults. Opposite the main entrance to the church there are seven small apses where various burial monuments of archbishops from Palermo are on display. Among these is the founder of the church himself, Gualtiero Offanilio.

The Cathedral

Palazzo dei Normanni (Palace of the Normans) also known as Palazzo Reale (Royal Palace) is a marvellous building constructed in Arab times in the 9th century. From the 11th century it was the royal residence of both Norman and Swabian nobility. It was renovated in the 14th century and hosted viceroys and members of the royal family from various European royal households. It has been the seat of the Assemblea Regionale Siciliana (Sicilian Regional Assembly) since 1947. Although the façade was transformed several times it still bears a distinctly 16th century air. Visitors can view the Palatina Chapel on the first floor and the royal apartments on the second floor of the palace.

Palazzo dei Normanni (The Palace of the Normans)

The Cappella Palatina (The Palatina Chapel) is undoubtedly one of the finest examples of Norman art that can be found in Palermo. It was built by order of Ruggero II in 1132 and consecrated eight years later. The central nave *inside* he chapel shows a splendid wooden ceiling in the typically "stalactite" style of Arabic art (circa *1143*). The floor is a beautiful expanse of mosaic and precious marbles have been used to embellish *the* lower half of the walls. Not far from the sanctuary stands a splendid ambo decorated with mosaics and supported by columns. An enormous 4.5 metre chandelier hangs from the ceiling and is delicately engraved with acanthus leaf motifs, human figures and animals. The nave walls and the sanctuary are *beautifully* decorated with splendid mosaics on a gold background showing the exotic influence of Byzantine style. A long the aisles there are beautiful wall paintings representing scenes from the lives of St.

The Palatina Chapel

Peter and St. Paul and from the Old Testament. In the Dome sanctuary you can admire the *Cristo Pantocratore* surrounded by angels and archangels while prophets, saints and evangelists line the pendentives and drum. A representation of the benediction of Christ embellishes the apse basin.

The royal apartments are of great interest to the visitor and include the Sala del Parlamento (Hall of Parliament) otherwise known as Sala d'Ercole (Hall of Hercules) which displays frescoes painted by Giuseppe Velasquez (18th - 19th centuries) and is used by the Sicilian Regional Assembly for its meetings. The Sala di Re Ruggero (Hall of King Roger) is decorated with mosaic representations of hunting scenes and dates back to 1170 circa. The Sala del Vicerè (Viceroy Hall) is lined with the portraits of illustrious Sicilian lieutenants. The dining room is divided by a vault supported by Gothic arches that rest on angular columns. Today, an astronomical observatory occupies the Pisana tower of the original treasury which is surrounded by aisles covered by majestic vaults overhead. Above this area there were the private apartments belonging to the Normans, adorned with splendid mosaics and illuminated by spacious windows.

The guards' rooms lie to the south of each tower. *Villa Bonanno*, a beautiful garden adorned with palm trees and containing the ruins of a Roman house, extends in front of the Palazzo dei Normanni.

Detail of the ceiling in the Sala di Ruggero

S. Giovanni degli Eremiti. The church of San Giovanni degli Eremiti in Via dei Benedettini is situated in an evocative garden full of exotic plants. It was built at the beginning of the 12th century by order of Ruggero II and was reconstructed in the second half of the last century. It is a typical example of Muslim architecture realised by Arab craftsmen. The austere bell towers, by comparison show the simple structure of eastern influence with lateral windows with one light and are crowned by a small, red dome, giving the whole building in its diversity of style an oriental touch. Inside, there are few adornments and the extreme simplicity of the interior is broken up only by the two great Gothic arches which cross over the only nave. The transept shows a group of three apses decorated with semicircular designs. The marvellous cloister which also dates back to the Norman period (13th century) was part of an ancient Benedictine monastery. It encloses a small garden surrounded by a series of Gothic archways supported by elegant couplets of small columns.

Professa House was built between 1564 and 1633. The interior is a marvellous example of Sicilian Baroque art showing an abundance of marble engravings, stuccowork, sculptures and paintings.

The Oratory of Saint Lawrence in Via della Immacolatella, contains rich decorations and stucco-work depicting scenes from the lives of St. Lawrence and St. Francis by Serpotta who has been described as "the greatest Sicilian sculptor of the 18th cent.". His vivacity and maturity come out in his work. Unfortunately the *Birth of Jesus* by Caravaggio (1609) was stolen from the alter.

San Giovanni degli Eremiti

One of the most impressive churches of the 13th century is the **Church of Saint Francis of Assisi** which overlooks the square bearing the same name. It is of a Gothic style and has a nave and two aisles decorated with allegorical statues by Serpotta in the central aisle. Both Gothic and Renaissance chapels can be seen in the lateral aisles. The fourth nave has a particularly striking entrance archway by Francesco Laurana and Pietro de Bontade (1468). In the right hand apse the Chapel dell'Immacolata can be admired for its polychrome marble engravings and 17th century sculptures by Ragusa. In the presbytery there is a most beautiful wooden choir dating back to 1524. The church known as **the Magione** looks onto a square which bears its name. It is dedicated to the Holy Trinity and encloses a beautiful garden. From the outside it is easy to see the distinctive Norman style of architecture. In fact the remains of the original Norman cloister can still be seen to the left of the nave showing the characteristic couplets of columns.

The Magione

Abatellis Palace in via Alloro has been used as the site of the **National Sicilian Gallery** since 1954 and displays pictures and sculptures from the National Museum. It is of late Gothic style and built following a project by Matteo Carnevalieri in 1490-95. It has a square plan with an inner courtyard surrounded by a double-arched porch. The façade is flanked at each corner by two towers with windows with two lights. The Gallery is laid out on two floors and occupies the porch and sixteen stairs. Among some of the most important works of art in this collection are the *Flight to Egypt* by the school of Antonello Gagini (1495), attributed to Laurana, the *The Triumph of Death* by the school of Pisanello, an earthenware jar of Hispanic-Arab origin painted white with gold decorations (13th - 14th cent.) that was brought up from the bottom of the sea near Palermo, the bust of Eleanor of Aragon by Laurana (1471), L'Annunziata by Antonello of Messina (1473), a *triptych by Malvagna di Mause* dating back to 1510, a *Madonna and child* also known as Lo Steri in piazza Marina is a Medieval construction from 1306 - 1380 erected by the powerful Chiaromonte family. The Sicilian

Bust of Eleanor of Aragon
(Francesco Laurana)

Houses of Parliament were also housed here in the 16th century and the Sant'Uffizio and other courts were held here up until 1960. The building looks down on piazza Marina with its central garden (Giardino Garibaldi) full of rare plants.

Virgin Annunziata
(by Antonello of Messina)

Abatellis palace

Archaeological Museum: this museum is housed in the House of the Philippean Fathers of the Olivella and possesses a rich assortment of underwater finds from the west of Sicily. Among these are sculptures of Egyptian and Punic origin, material from the Roman times from the towns of Tindari and Solunto and lion-headed guttering from the Himera temple (Sala Marconi). Sculptures discovered during excavations are on exhibition in the Sala di Selinunte and include four metopes representing the Delfic Triad (Artemis, Latona and Apollo), a winged sphinx, a European rat and Hercules fighting a bull dating back to 580 B.C. There are also three metopes from temple C, that represent the four figures of Apollo, Perseus and the Medusa, Heracles and the Cercopis, four metopes from temple E depicting Hercules fighting against the Amazonian, the marriage between Zeus and Hera, Atheon being punished by Artemis and Atha fighting against Encelado. The bronze statue of Efebus from Selinunte from the 5th century B.C. is on show in the middle of the room and to round off the exhibition there is a fine assortment of finds from Chiusi in the Etruscan Collection among which you can see burial stones, sculptures and sarcophagi. On the first floor you can visit rooms showing finds of various kinds from different localities around Sicily. In the Sala dei Bronzi (Bronze Room) a variety of bronze statues of Greek, Etruscan and Roman origin are on display and among these are two pieces of particular importance, the *Aries* from the Maniace Castle in Syracuse (3rd cent. B.C.) and the *Athlete Killing a Deer*, which is the huge mouth of a fountain from Pompei. On the second floor there is a large collection of prehistoric material from around Sicily. Also on this floor are Greek ceramics, paintings and mosaics from Salunto and Palermo and interesting finds from the Himera excavations. The Neo-classical architecture can be seen at its best in the **Teatro Massimo** and the **Politeama Garibaldi**. The Massimo theatre designed by Basile in 1875 is one of the most important in Europe. Basile's son, Ernesto finished the work his father had started, two years later. The ample façade with its Corinthian style pronaos and staircase constitute one of the most sophisticated examples of architecture inspired by classicism. Inspired by Pompean style, the **Politeama Garibaldi** erected by Giuseppe Damiani Almeyda in 1874 has its top storey crowned with high relief motifs and embellished with a bronze quadriga by Mario Rutelli. The room on the top floor of the Politeama houses the Civic Gallery of Modern Art.

Hercules
Killing a deer

The Teatro Massimo

The Politeama Garibaldi Theatre

Church of Saint Domenic

The Oratorio di S. Zita (Oratory of St. Zita) at number 3, Via Valverde can be reached through a side entrance to the left of the S. Zita church. The whole of the interior was decorated by Giacomo Serpotta between 1686 and 1718 and the walls are all covered with allegorical statues and high-relief sculptures among which the *"Mysteries"* and the "Battle of Lepanto" are represented.

La Chiesa di S. Domenico (St. Dominic's Church) was built in the 14th century but was rebuilt in Baroque style in 1636. The façade is typical of late Renaissance style with its Baroque cornice and scroll decorations.

The Palazzo della Zisa overlooking the square which bears its name was begun by order of the Norman King Guglielmo I (William I) and completed by his son Guglielmo II (William *II*). Annexed to the church is a convent with the catacombs used

Palazzo della Zisa

by the Cappuccini monks. **The Catacombe dei Cappuccini** also looks out onto a square named after it. It was built in the first few years of the 18th century. Despite the renovations that were carried out at the beginning of the century many 18th century works of art such as the wooden alters, paintings, funeral monuments and even a rare collection of bookshave survived. The Catacombs are famous for the 8,000 skeletons, mummies and preserved bodies which represent the deceased of the upper social classes who, from the 16th century onwards practised the art of mummification in order to preserve the bodies of their loved ones for posterity. The practice was discontinued after a long period because it was thought too macabre.

Chinese Palace

The Favorita Park at the foot of the Pellegrino Mountains, north-west of the city can be reached from via Duca degli Abruzzi. It was created in 1799 by Ferdinand III of Bourbon when, having been defeated by the French in Naples he fled to Sicily. As you enter the park one of the first sights to catch the eye is the **Palazzina Cinese** (Chinese Palace) built on a project by Venanzio Marvuglia which reflected the fashion of that period in its neoclassical structure overlaid by Chinese style roofs and pinnacles. It is a typical marriage of different styles of architecture featuring Gothic arches reaching the ground, classical balconies and Liberty turrets. Not far from here is the **Museo Etnografico Pitrè** (Ethnographic Museum) which has an interesting collection of artefacts which illustrate the customs and traditions of the Sicilian people. The puppet theatre and the collection of Baroque statues from the nativity scene are particularly interesting.

Monte Pellegrino. This 606 metre high mountain dominates the sky-line over the city of Palermo. A long winding path up the steep sides of the mountain offers the visitor a breathtaking view of the whole city and the Conca d'Oro. **The Santuario di S. Rosalia** (Sanctuary of St. Rosalia) consists of a convent and a small chapel carved out of the mountainside, where Saint Rosalia lived a life of penance until her death in 1166. Saint Rosalia is the patron Saint and protector of the city where she has been venerated since the 17th century when the city was freed from the plague thanks to her divine intervention. Her chapel, dug out of the rock reaches back under the mountainside to a depth of about 25 metres. The walls ooze water which is thought to have miraculous powers. A statue of the saint can be seen under the alter, clothed in a cloak of silver and gold and dates back to the 17th century. The chapel has become a place of pilgrimage for the people of Palermo. In a small courtyard in front of the convent visitors can see a statue of Saint Rosalia.

Mondello, which lies between Mount Pellegrino and Mount Gallo near Palermo is one of the most prestigious seaside resorts in Sicily.

The oldest part situated on the most northern point of the bay is inhabited by fishermen. The only surviving part of what was once an ancient castle is a single tower which looks out onto the bay. The area was developed with the construction of villas at the turn of the century transforming the city into a green belt. However the height of its expansion took place between the two World Wars when it became a residential area for people from Palermo who spent most of the year here. Only after the Second World War did Mondello become a commuter-town for the masses.

Mondello

The island of Ustica lies 36 miles off the north coast of Palermo. Its volcanic origins give it its elliptic shape which measures 8.6 sq. km.

A landscape of petrified lava gives the island a wild appearance which has earned it the name of Black Pearl of the Mediterranean Sea. In fact, the name Ustica is derived from the Latin word "ustum" which means "burnt".

The town of Ustica with its picturesque houses decorated with murals by famous contemporary artists rises on the side of a tuffaceous hill.

The Museum of Underwater Archaeology is housed in St. Mary's tower and contains the remains of old shipwrecks and the lost city of Osteodes.

Clear waters, the abundance of fish and numerous grottoes dotted a long the coastline make Ustica a haven for underwater fishermen.

Segesta

Segesta is an important archaeological centre in the west of Sicily near Calatafimi on the edge of Mount Barbaro. It was originally inhabited by the Celims, descendants of the Trojans who were constantly at war with the people of Salunte. Under Carthaginian rule the city once again entered into battle against Selinunte later allying itself with the Romans at the beginning of the Punic War. The Romans used the city as a strategic vantage point for its army.

The Vandals, however managed to completely destroy the city de-

spite its double city walls which run all the way round it. Although the city has never been thoroughly excavated you can see the theatre and the Doric Temple quite clearly.

The Theatre is only building visible within the city walls, it dates back to the Hellenistic Age to the 4th or 5th century. The stairway and the stage were renovated by the Romans. The theatre faces north, perhaps to look out onto the Castellammare Gulf and has twenty steps carved out of the rock which form the "cavea" or gallery.

The Temple dates back to the 5th century. It is built outside the city walls on a flat mountain slope. Its evocative position and its excellent state of repair make it a fascinating building to visit. Three steps lead up to a Doric peristyle of 16 columns that support the entablement and two front pieces. The naos and the roof are missing, perhaps because the temple was used for open-air worship.

Doric Temple

Segesta

The Agora

Greek Theatre

The Church

Mediaeval Castle

Sanctuary

Dello Zingaro Nature Reserve

Dwarf palm

The parklands of the Dello Zingaro nature reserve extend north of Scopello towards steep, white cliffs peppered with caves and grottoes. It was founded in 1981 and covers an area of about 1,600 hectares rich in natural vegetation. To get to the reserve visitors have to walk through a wide tunnel bored through the rock which was originally intended to be the entrance to a panoramic pathway that linked Scopello and S. Vito Lo Capo but is actually a well made path that runs from Cala Mazzo di Sciacca to la Torre dell'Impiso (The Tower of the Hanged Man) on the other side of the reserve. A long the pathway which, though well maintained, can be rather steep in places, visitors can admire surprisingly beautiful countryside and note the abundance of dwarf palm trees which constitute the most common type of vegetation on the island. **The Grotto dell'Uzzo** lies just beyond Cala Marinella and was used even in prehistoric times as a shelter. Now visitors can see a quaint fishing village and the remains of an ancient tower. Not far from here you can see the Tonnarella dell'Uzzo (tuna processing plant) where rare fish called "long wings" similar to tunny fish were caught.

Beach of the Uzzo

The tunny-fishing port of Scopello

Scopello. The delightful position of this town has made it a favourite tourist spot and has encouraged the building of holiday-houses.

The tunny-fishing port in the little bay is guarded by two picturesque rocks which stick up out of the sea and is watched over by the coast guard tower. Of great interest is the industrial plant for the processing of tunny fish which was already in existence in 1580. You can visit the plant and see the beams, offices, even the chapel and the storehouses practically all in tact.

Saint Vito lo Capo lies in a sandy valley at the foot of Mount Monaco. Its clear waters and sandy beach make it an attractive holiday resort for tourists. The Chiesa Madre dating back to the 17th century and the lighthouse on Cape San Vito are worth visiting.

San Vito Lo Capo

Erice

Erice is one of the most picturesque towns on the island. Visitors can feel the Medieval air of the place, as they walk down its narrow lanes and across its cobbled squares. The architecture is typically Medieval in flavour, however its origins reach further back to when Venus Ericina, goddess of fertility was worshipped at the temple dedicated to her. The town was inhabited by the Helims, the Chartheginians and the Romans. It bore the name of *Monte San Giuliano* given to it by the Normans under whose rule the town flourished until 1934. The city walls form a triangle on which the ruins of the temple, *Pepoli Castle* renovated at the turn of the century and the Gothic *Matrice* church can still be seen. The Chiesa Matrice conserves an original Madonna by Laurana.

The Civic Museum A. Cordici in piazza Umberto I as many exhibits of interest among which are Aphrodite's Head from the 4th century B.C. a

The church Matrice

Characteristic alley

painting of *The Annunciation* by Gagini from 1525 and a painting by A. Carrera of *Mary Magdalen and Martha.* The original city walls are still standing and in good condition. A long the length of the walls small turrets, four-sided strongholds and three city gates which are *Sword Gate, Gate of Carmen* and *Trapani Gate* may still be seen. These gates were rebuilt by the Normans in the 12th century on the original 5th century perimeter established by the Cartheginians and the Romans. **Saint John the Baptist Church** is situated in piazza S. Giovanni. It is of Medieval origin but was refurbished in the 17th century and holds the statue of *S. Giovanni Evangelista* by Antonino Gagini on the main alter and also a 4th century sculpture by an unknown artist of the *Virgin Mary and Saint Elizabeth.*

The Balio Gardens lie on the site of an ancient acropolis where the temple of Venus Ericina once stood. Here too, visitors can drop in on the **Scientific Cultural Centre Ettore Majorana** in Via Guarnotta directed by Prof. Zichichi of international renown.

Castle of Balio or Pepoli

Trapani

Trapani lies in the shadow of Mount Erice and extends towards the sea. It seems that the first inhabitants of this city came from the Ionian coast and were probably Sicani from Drepano. It was also inhabited by the Helims who founded Egesta, Erice and Entella and the Phoenicians. The old city centre has a distinctly Arabic style about its streets, squares and buildings. Visitors can see some monuments from the Renaissance and Baroque periods at the churches of St. Dominic's, St. Michael's and Palazzo Chiaramonte. Palazzo della Giudecca is a prime example of 16th century architecture with its large wedge shaped portal and its ashlar tower. The Santuario dell'Annunziata is, in contrast an example of Gothic style with the addition of a Baroque bell-tower.

The Pepoli National Museum holds great works of art by the great masters among which are Gagini and in the art gallery there are paintings by Tiziano and Caraciolo to mention a few. Visitors will enjoy watching the spectacular tunny fishing here and there is also an interesting salt deposit that has been turned into a national nature reserve under the direction of the conservationist group W.W.F. In the **Salt Museum** you can see the artefacts and objects used to collect and transport salt. One of the most famous and colourful religious festivals of this area is called la processione dei Misteri (Procession of the Mysteries).

Island of the Colombaia

The salt deposits

A windmill

A windmill

Panorama

55

Egadi Islands

The Egadi islands of Levanzo, Favignana, Marettimo and the tiny island of Maraona and Formica, form an archipelago that lies off the Trapanese coast. During the Punic Wars they were the scene of many bloody battles and witnessed the victory of the Romans over the Cartheginians.

Favignana is the largest island and lies 17 km. from the mainland. The main town is situated on the north coast and it has a small harbour guarded by the Saint Giacomo Fortress, Florio castle and the Saint Catherine Fortress.

The waters around this island afford an ideal habitat for the yellow-fin tunny fish for which it is famous. The transparent waters and idyllic grottoes are a great tourist attraction.

Cala Rossa (Red bay)

Cala Azzurra (Azure bay)

Levanzo is the nearest island to the coast of Trapani and measures 10 km. sq. It has inaccessibly rocky cliffs around its coast which contain caves of prehistoric interest. One of these caves called the Grotta del Genovese has a unique display of Paleolithic and Neolithic art depicting human figures and animals on the cave walls. Inland, there is a large flat plain where grapes and corn are grown.

The mountainous island of **Marettimo** is the furthest away from the Trapani coast and measures 12 km. sq. At its centre an austere Fortress which was used by the Bourbons as a prison looms up against the skyline.

Visitors can hire boats to see the many interesting caves and grottoes that are dotted around the island's coastline.

Pantelleria

The island of **Pantelleria** is situated 110km. from Mazara del Vallo and 70 km. from Tunisia. Many finds dating back to the Neolithic period have been excavated on the island, such as the "*sesi*" (dome-shaped burial chambers) which vaguely resemble the nuraghi in Sardinia. Its volcanic origins can be seen manifested in the *Montagna Grande* a now extinct volcanic crater surrounded by 24 minor craters known as the Cuddie dai monti Gibelé and the Cuddie Attalora. The last eruption was registered in 1891 but the presence of "Favore" (hot water jets that shoot up from between the *cracks in the rock surface), the dry baths or "stufe" (steam-filled rocky caverns), the "mofete" (carbon* dioxide leaks) and the "bukire" (wells of brackish water) testify to the volcanic energy trapped beneath the surface. The islands economy is based on the cultivation of capers and the zibibbo grape used to make sultanas and also sweet dessert wines. The main places of interest to the tourist are Pantelleria, Khamma, Tracino and Scauri. Scattered all over the slopes of the rocky island are the traditional "dammusi" which are the typical white, cube-shaped houses with tiny windows. There is an old castle at Pantelleria called the Barbacane which you can visit. Visitors can make a tour of the island either on land or by sea to reach the many marine grottoes some of which are only accessible *by boat.*

Arco dell'Elefante (Elephant Arch)

Dammuso a traditional house

Specchio di Venere Lake

Mozía

Legend has it that Mozia was founded by Hercules but historically its birth has been traced back to the Phoenicians who were the first to give this Sicilian colony the name of Mozia which means "Spinning Mill".

Later it came under the domination of Carthage and for many years was involved in the wars between Carthage and Greece for possession of the island. In 397 it was conquered by Dioniges I of Syracuse but was later retaken by the Cartheginians who transferred the population to Lilibeo.

After this date nothing more is known about the historical development of this area. Joseph Whitaker, an English historian was the first to unearth the ruins of Mozia bringing to light a large part of the ancient town. His daughter continued his research and their villa is now the site of a museum.

Not far from the museum there is a house built to a Greek design on the original site of a Phoenician house with an inner courtyard. The floors of this courtyard are covered with small black and white stones arranged to depict animals fighting each other and surrounded by a columned porch in Doric style.

The old sunken road that used to link the island with Birgi, across the Stagnone, built out of rubble in the 6th century to transport grapes from vineyards on the island to the winemaker's, may still be seen at low tide. The artificial road was used up until a few years ago.

Youth of Motya

The cothon

Marsala was founded by the Carthaginians at the end of the 4th century B.C. but was lost to the Romans and later the Saracens. In fact the name Marsala is a corruption of the Saracen name "Marsa Allah" which means (God's Gate). A succession of invaders took possession of the island after the Saracens, the Normans, the Angevins, the Arroganese and the Bourbons.

Punic ship

On 11th May 1860 Garibaldi and his army of one thousand (Mille) arrived on Sicily to liberate the island. In the 18th century an enterprising businessman by the name of John Woodhouse discovered the commercial value of the excellent wines produced in this area. His initiative opened the floodgates for international wine trading and many of the original wine-making plants like Ingham (1804) and Florio (1831) can still be seen. Other places of interest are the 17th century Municipal Palace, the Dome, the church of S. Giovanni and the Lilibeo National Museum showing an interesting exhibition of the remains of a Punic shipwreck dating back to the 3rd cent. B.C. Also dating from the 3rd cent. is the so called "Insula Romana" an area of particular archaeological interest where you can see thermal baths and polychrome mosaics.

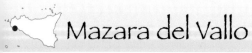

Mazara del Vallo

Mazara looks out over the harbour canal at the mouth of the Mazzaro river. It is the heart of the wine-producing and fishing industries boasting the largest fleet of fishing-boats in Italy. Founded by the Phoenicians it was occupied by a succession of conquering civilizations, the Cartheginians, the Romans in Medieval times the Arabs and the Normans who all left their distinctive mark on the architecture. A prime example of Arabo-Norman building can be seen in constructions such as St. Nicholas Regal with its square shape and merlons along the top.

The Cathedral built in the 11th century was restored in the 17th century and shows a magnificent high relief detail of Count Ruggero triumphing over his fallen enemy. The façade is divided into three parts. In the lower part two high plinths emphasise the central doorway in typical 17th century style with a Roman arch supported by two slender columns connected to an arched entablature.

The second series of columns is almost an extension of the lower row, having four symmetrical Doric semi-columns inside which there are two statues, one of *Christ* and one of the *Madonna.* In the third row a round window surrounded by ornamental friezes and supported by two angels on ornate panels can be seen. Inside the nave is a systematic series of Roman arches supported on Doric columns. The main alter in white marble, stands below the cupola and is raised on three steps where there is a Baroque tabouret. The vaulting above the central aisle is richly decorated with a representation of the *"The Triumph of Faith, Hope and Charity"* in the centre while to the south side you can see the *"Apocalypse"* and on the north side the *"Jacob's Dream"*.

The four cardinal virtues are represented on the lunettes, Justice, Strength, Prudence and Temperance.

You can see the statue of Saint Vito in the main piazza embellished by 18th century masonry. It was created by Marabitti in the second half of the 18th cent.

Selinunte is a must on the agenda of any visitor who really wants to discover ancient Sicily. The ruins of this city lie evocatively in beautiful surroundings on the south east coast, at the mouth of the River Madione, in the Castelvetrano area.

It was originally founded by the Greeks of Megara Iblea in the second half of the 7th century B.C. Its name "Selinon" means wild parsley in the Greek language, and was given to the area because of the abundance of this particular plant. Numerous Greek coins with the emblem of this plant have been discovered here. After a turbulent relationship with Segesta it was destroyed repeatedly by the Cartheginians in 409 and again in 250. It sustained the destruction of an earthquake in the Byzantine period which reduced it to ruins. Despite being used as a deposit of building materials for the local population some very interesting remains have survived, such as the eastern temples and the acropolis dedicated to a god whose name though inscribed on numerous stones is illegible.

As was the custom in those times all the buildings face east.

Temple E

Temple E

Selinunte

Temple C

The oldest and largest temple is **Temple C**. It has a hexastyle form with 42 columns and is very similar in construction to the Temple of Apollo in Syracuse. Work on this huge building was begun in 530 B.C. and never completed because of the destruction of the city by an earthquake.

The once walled **Acropolis** now only has a small part of its outer walls in tact, however its network of roads with its two main streets crossing each other at a perpendicular angle can still give us an idea of the urban plan of the city.

Temple F

Temple G

Within the city boundaries **Temples O and A** date back to the Punic times.
The Melaphoros Sanctuary was built on a hill in the first half of the 6th century B.C. on the site of a much older temple. It possesses two alters one smaller, older one and one used for sacrifices as the epigraph dedicated to the goddess Demetra "Portatrice del Melograno" (Bearer of Pomegranates) shows. Moving in a northerly direction you come to another sanctuary or shrine called the **Santuario of Zeus Meilichios** (Sanctuary of Zeus Meilichios).

Temple A

View of the harbour

Sciacca is a well known spa and seaside resort which lies on a flat coastal plain that drops sheer to the sea between the river Platani and Belice estuaries. It was originally founded in Roman times by the people of Selinunte and was later invaded by the Arabs in the 9th century who changed its name from *Thermae Selinuntinae to Sciacca.*

The Norman occupation of 1087 gave way to the forces of Guglielmo Peralta one of four deputies of the island in 1355.

The castle he had built is still in existence today. In the 16th century the Luna family took over beginning a period of decline which was to last almost two hundred years because of civil disputes.

The lower half of the city runs parallel to the sea behind the harbour while its centre focuses on piazza Scandaliato which looks out onto the sea.

The higher part of the city reaches up as far as the original 16th century walls where the new area of the town has grown following a criss-cross plan.

The piazza Scandaliato is surrounded by trees and overlooks the sea and the harbour below. At the opposite end of is the *Town Hall* once a Jesuit Convent in 1615.

The 13th century Dome was completely restored in the 18th century retaining only three original apses while the Baroque façade was never completed. Inside and outside statues by the sculptors Antonino and Gian Domenico Gagini can be seen.

The Selinuntine Spa of Saint Calogero situated a long the sea front near the Saint Calogero Sanctuary offers different types of water for the cure of various ailments. It is made up of two main buildings, the new spa plant (*Stabilimento delle Nuove Terme*) and the steam bath area (*Stabilimento delle Stufe*).

The spa and the Cammordino promontory

Seccagrande

Eraclea Minoa is situated near Capo Bianco on the road that links Sciacca to the city of Agrigento on the other side of the river Platani. In the 6th century B.C. it was christened *Minoia* by the people of Selinunte. The Spartans who took possession of the town to gain a vantage point from which they could threaten the Cartheginians, called it Eraclea. Between the 5th and 3rd centuries B.C. the area together with other Greco-Sicilian towns were a battle zone for these two civilizations. The Romans had the victory after the Second Punic War when they repossessed the land. It was then abandoned, once more, at the end of the 1st century. Recent excavations carried out in the area have unearthed a 4th century city wall made of chalk blocks, a circular tower and a square shaped tower. **The Theatre** has to be one of the most important monuments. Facing the sea, the terraces offer a large seating capacity ten steps high and divided into nine sections. There is also a **museum** which houses various finds from the excavation on display inside.

Scala dei Turchi (Staircase of the Turks)

The Greek Theatre

Pelagie Islands

This group of islands consist of Linosa, Lampedusa and Lampione and can be reached by boat from the Port of Empedocle. Lampedusa can also be reached by air from Palermo and other cities.

Linosa is a square shaped island of volcanic origin. It has patches of greenery and no running surface water. There is one small village on the island.

Lampedusa, the biggest of the three islands has sporadic clumps of vegetation and few streams. Its main economy is based on the fishing industry and the gathering of natural sea-sponges apart from tourism.

You can see some remains of Phoenician, Greek, Roman and Arab constructions, however the island was uninhabited until Ferdinand II of Bourbon established a colony there.
Lampione is a rock inhabited only by seagulls.

Linosa

Lampedusa - The beach and Conigli (Rabbits) Island

Agrigento

Agrigento affords a magnificent panorama from its well-favoured position on the top of two hills that stand side by side. From here you can see the Temple Valley and the sea. It was founded in 580 under the name of *Akragas* on a site previously inhabited in prehistoric times. Its domain extended as far as the north coast of Sicily. The Arabs changed its name to *Girgenti* in the 4th century but it was not until 1927 that its present name of Agrigento was officially recognised. Among the famous people born here there is the 5th century Philosopher Empedocles and the famous writer *Luigi Pirandello* (1867 - 1936). A mild climate creates ideal conditions for the thriving of plants such as the almond tree which flowers in the middle of winter creating a beautiful display for visitors to see. Via Atenea is one of the most popular locations for the traditional afternoon walk and if you want to buy a souvenir of the island the "gargarnarruni" or "scacciapensieri" a small musical instrument known as a "worry soother" is what you must ask for.

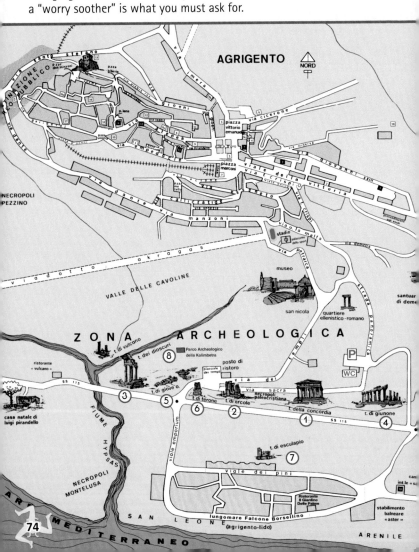

The Valley of the Temples is celebrated from December to March with village fairs and folk dancing. The blossoming almond trees add to the magic atmosphere against the background of the majestic Temples of Juno Lacinia, of Concord, of Hercules, of Castor and Pollux and of Jove. The Temple of Hercules dates back to the 6th century B.C. To reach the *Temple of Jove of Olympus* you have to follow Via Francesco Crispi until you get to the piazza in front of the temple. The Norman church, *Chiesa di S. Biagio* (Church of St. Biagio) is situated in Via Demetra and was built on top of the ruins of the Temple of Demetra (480, 460 B.C.). The church occupies the apsidiole or cella of the original temple and uncovers the apse and the pronao.

The Temple of Castor and Polluce

View of the Valley of the Temples

Agrigento

The Temple of Concord is a marvel of architectural harmony and proportion and has survived the test of time much better than the other temples. It was built in about 450 B.C. and is a hexastyle rectangle surrounded by 34 columns on a basement of four steps.

① The Temple of Concord

The Temple of Hercules was built at the end of the 6th century on a podium going up three steps with 38 columns are erected. Just south of the Temple near **Porta Aurea** is the 1st century **Tomb of Terone** a small two- storey burial monument on a square base, which dates back to Roman times.

Of **The Temple Castor and Pollux** at the centre of the sanctuary dedicated to the Ctonie gods is made up of a group of 4 columns that have now become the symbolic emblem of Agrigento.

The Temple of Juno stands alone on the cliff and dates back to 450 B.C. It has a columned porch which runs all the way round the exterior, six frontal columns on a base with four steps.

Outside the **Temple of Jove of Olympus** there is a carpark from which you can walk to the Temple. Similar in size to the temple at Selinunte it was built to celebrate the Roman victory over the Chartheginians at Imera in 480. It was a pseudoperisphere with a wall interrupted by half-columns instead of the traditional peristyle. Holding up the heavy entablature there used to be four enormous *telamons* 7.65 metres high. The mark left by one of the latter can be seen on the ground in the centre of the ruin. The original telemon is now kept in *the Regional Archaeological Museum*.

⑤ The telemon

⑥ The Tomb of Terone

⑧ Kolimbetra garden

On the banks of the River Akragas you can see the ruins of the **Temple of Aesculapius** from the 5th century.

⑦ The Temple of Aesculapius

The Church of S. Nicola (Church of St. Nicholas) was built by the Cistercian monks using material taken from nearby ruins. It has a beautiful portal set in a Roman arch with a simple yet stately façade. It is an aisle-less church and in the second chapel on the right hand side you can see a sarcophagus engraved with scenes from the *myth of Fedra and Hyppolytus* dating back to the 2nd century A.D. inspired by Greek mythology. You can enjoy a magnificent view of the temples from the church.

The Falaride Oratory situated to the left of the church, is a wonderful example of late Hellenistic architecture. It is thought to have been the tomb of a Roman lady from the 1st century A.D. but in actual fact, it was a small temple built on the site, as legend would have it, near the palace belonging to Falaride the first tyrant of Agrigento.

You can get to the **Regional Archaeological Museum** through the cloisters inside the church of S. Nicola. The museum houses numerous important exhibits in various rooms. In the first room panels showing ancient documents about Agrigento and ancient town plans are on display. In *Room* 2 prehistoric remains found in the area together with ancient Greek finds concerning the foundation of *Akragas* are on show.

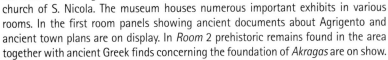

The Oratory of Falaride

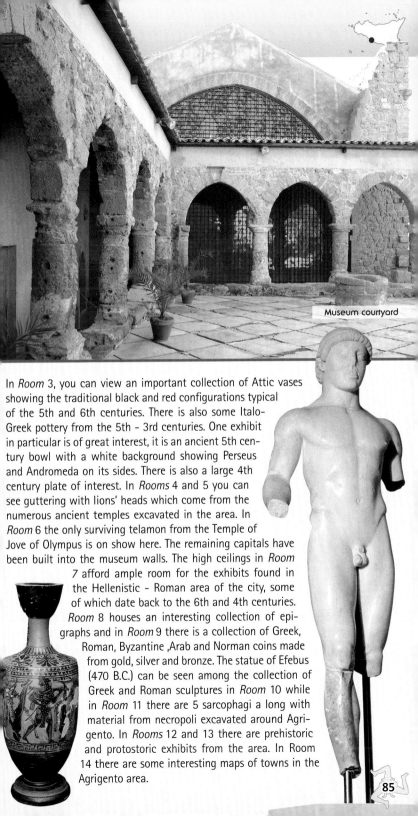

Museum courtyard

In *Room* 3, you can view an important collection of Attic vases showing the traditional black and red configurations typical of the 5th and 6th centuries. There is also some Italo-Greek pottery from the 5th - 3rd centuries. One exhibit in particular is of great interest, it is an ancient 5th century bowl with a white background showing Perseus and Andromeda on its sides. There is also a large 4th century plate of interest. In *Rooms* 4 and 5 you can see guttering with lions' heads which come from the numerous ancient temples excavated in the area. In *Room* 6 the only surviving telamon from the Temple of Jove of Olympus is on show here. The remaining capitals have been built into the museum walls. The high ceilings in *Room* 7 afford ample room for the exhibits found in the Hellenistic - Roman area of the city, some of which date back to the 6th and 4th centuries. *Room* 8 houses an interesting collection of epigraphs and in *Room* 9 there is a collection of Greek, Roman, Byzantine ,Arab and Norman coins made from gold, silver and bronze. The statue of Efebus (470 B.C.) can be seen among the collection of Greek and Roman sculptures in *Room* 10 while in *Room* 11 there are 5 sarcophagi a long with material from necropoli excavated around Agrigento. In *Rooms* 12 and 13 there are prehistoric and protostoric exhibits from the area. In Room 14 there are some interesting maps of towns in the Agrigento area.

85

In *Room* 15 there is an interesting display of photographs of finds excavated in Gela. In the middle of the room there is a beautiful red bowl showing pictures of *Amazons* around it which dates back to the 5th century. In *Rooms* 16 and 17 there are maps of Nisseno and Caltanisetta and finally to round off the exhibition, in *Room* 18 there is a collection of miscellaneous items.

In **the Roman/Hellenic part of the city,** which you can get to by following the main road through a gateway, there are four main streets lined with Italo - Hellenic style houses which were once both homes and shops. Traces of painted plaster and mosaic flooring from the 2nd and 3rd centuries can still be distinguished. One of the most striking features of the Medieval part of the city is the **Abbazia di S. Spirito** (Abbey of the Holy Spirit) which dates back to the 13th century which has been completely restored. the church interior was renovated in the 18th century and shows a beautiful wooden ceiling with stucco-work by Giacomo Serpotta. The entrance to the old monastery is on the right side of the church and is distinctly Medieval in style, as is the cloister surrounded by Gothic portals, *the refectory*, now the site of the Municipal Library and the *main hall*.

Roman/Hellenistic district

The church known as the **Chiesa del Purgatorio** has a magnificent Baroque church door. It contains some beautiful stucco-work and the famous statues of the "Virtues" by the artist Giacomo Serpotta. In the Civic Museum, which is situated in the town square you can see some Medieval sculptures and paintings dating from the 14th to the 18th centuries, among which Luca Giordani's *Satyr chasing a Nymph* can be admired. **The Dome** built between the 13th and 14th centuries, has been repeatedly renovated. Its belfry shows a double row of blind tracery windows and a Arab-Norman style balcony. Inside it has a nave with two aisles and a lacunar ceiling constructed with recessed panels. The *Chapel of Saint Gerlando* is of interest as it holds the relics of the patron saint of the city. An interesting phenomenon due to the architectural structure of the presbytery occurs here, whereby even a whisper uttered at the entrance of the Dome can be heard quite distinctly by people standing in the apse. **The Archbishop's Sanctuary** has a beautiful courtyard surrounded by Baroque columns. A *museum of Sacred Art* has been established in its grounds, where you can see frescoes, church art and sarcophagi.

Luigi Pirandello's birth place is situated 6km. from Agrigento. The Nobel Prize winner for Literature had his ashes preserved at the foot of a pine tree overlooking the sea. Unfortunately a freak wind badly damaged its branches on 7th November 1997.

The Cathedral

Pirandello's birth place

Enna is also known as "the umbilical chord of Sicily" because of its central position. It was a "Sican" settlement under the name of Henna which practised a similar religion to that of the cult of Demetra. In the period of Greek colonisation, it was attacked by the Syracusan general Agatocles in the 4th century and later also by Carthage. In the 2nd century it came under Roman rule and was violently repressed by its new masters as a punishment for a slave revolt. It became a "municipium" during the Imperial period and was conquered by the Byzantines after the fall of Rome. In 859 after a long seige the Arabs occupied the city giving it the name of Kasrlànna and bringing back prosperity to Enna, until the arrival of the Normans in the 6th century. The city, today is spread over the highest part of a mountainous offshoot which affords beautiful views. Most of the land is cultivated, but the area has enjoyed success as a tourist attraction because of its wonderful panorama.

Frederick's Tower

The 11th century Cathedral was built by the Aragonese but was badly damaged by fire in the 15th century. Restoration was not fully completed until the 17th century.

This massive building looks out onto a broad stairway flanked by a colonnade on which an impressive 17th century tower stands. The triple apse is of obvious Gothic influence and inside the nave and two aisles are intersected by mighty columns set in Gothic arches. A 16th century font can be seen in the north aisle together with the carved *scroll* sculpted by G. Gallina in the 17th century and also, a *baptismal font*. The wooden lacunar ceiling is of particular beauty.

The Lombardy Castle is an ancient building situated in the upper part of the city. It was built just before the Swabian period. It originally had twenty towers however, only six of these have survived. One of these is the **Pisana Tower** which has a merloned battlement.

Frederick's Tower is set on an octagonal base and is situated in the middle of the public gardens. It was built in the 13th century and was probably a part of a much larger and impressive castle.

Panorama

Piazza Armerina

Piazza Armerina is noted for its ancient Roman Villa, one of the most beautiful houses that has come down to us through the ages in tact. In 1161, Guglielmo I destroyed the city, which had sprung up around the Villa del Casale because it had welcomed rebellious barons, his enemies. The city, however was rebuilt on the original site. One of the most interesting times to visit Piazza Armina is in August, when the annual *Palio dei Normanni* (Festival of the Normans) takes place. **The Cathedral**, originally of Gothic construction, has undergone improvements over the centuries, those of 1604 being most evident today. The church dominates the city centre with its Baroque portal and the original Gothic - Catalan structure of the belfry. The main alter is embellished by the presence of a tabernacle with a stone table depicting the *Madonna della Vittoria* (Madonna of Victory). The chapel on the left contains a *crucifix* painted on both sides by a master known as Maestro della Croce di Piazza Armerina. There is also a 15th century *Vergine col bambino* (Virgin and Child).

The Cathedral

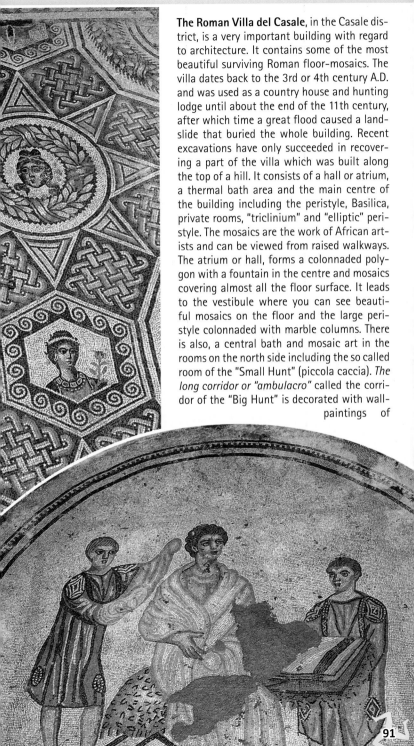

The Roman Villa del Casale, in the Casale district, is a very important building with regard to architecture. It contains some of the most beautiful surviving Roman floor-mosaics. The villa dates back to the 3rd or 4th century A.D. and was used as a country house and hunting lodge until about the end of the 11th century, after which time a great flood caused a landslide that buried the whole building. Recent excavations have only succeeded in recovering a part of the villa which was built along the top of a hill. It consists of a hall or atrium, a thermal bath area and the main centre of the building including the peristyle, Basilica, private rooms, "triclinium" and "elliptic" peristyle. The mosaics are the work of African artists and can be viewed from raised walkways. The atrium or hall, forms a colonnaded polygon with a fountain in the centre and mosaics covering almost all the floor surface. It leads to the vestibule where you can see beautiful mosaics on the floor and the large peristyle colonnaded with marble columns. There is also, a central bath and mosaic art in the rooms on the north side including the so called room of the "Small Hunt" (piccola caccia). *The long corridor or "ambulacro"* called the corridor of the "Big Hunt" is decorated with wallpaintings of

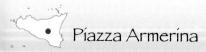
hunting scenes. The so called "Gymnasts' Room" is also known as the "*Room of the 10 Girls*" because of the mosaic images of scantily-dressed young girls, wearing something very similar to the modern bikini shown doing gymnastics. Not far from this point, there is a room with a central fountain where you can see Orpheus. In the east part of the corridor of the "Big Hunt" there is an assembly room and to the south you can see the zone of the building intended for living quarters which are beautifully decorated with mosaics. Many of the rooms on the east side of the villa are decorated with mythological characters and the elliptic *peristyle* is surround-

ed by a colonnade and has a fountain in the centre of the courtyard from which you can see the other mosaics in other rooms showing cupids fishing or gathering grapes. The "*triclinium*", also showing images from mythology, leads directly into the so called "*Sala del Circo*" or "Circus Room" depicting scenes of races held at the Circo Massimo in Rome. The original hypocaust system can still be seen in the *Tepidarium*, a room where you could bathe in tepid water, the *Calidarium* where you could bathe in hot water and lastly, *the Frigidarium* where you could refresh yourself with a cold water bath.

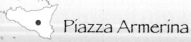

Morgantina is a large town on the slopes of the Erei Mountains famous for its Norman castle. There are many items of archaeological interest discovered on the site of the nearby Morgantina on show at the *"Antiquarium"*.

Excavation work has unearthed the *"Agora"* or meeting place, the *"Macellum"* or slaughter house, the *"Bauleuterion"*, the *"Ginnasio"* or gymnasium, the *"theatre"*, the ruins of a house, a *shrine* dedicated to the cult of the spirits from the Underworld and another dedicated to *Demetra* and *Kore*.

Caltagirone

Caltagirone is one of the most thriving towns inland. It lies in a picturesque setting on top of three neighbouring hills, two of which are joined by a monumental bridge. From this position the town dominates the Caltagirone and Maraglio valleys below. Excavations carried out in the Montagna area have unearthed the site of an ancient "Siculi" settlement dating back to the Bronze Age. Other digs have revealed the existence of a Greek town in the 6th century A.D. though, as yet nothing has been found to give us any information about Byzantine or Saracen Caltagirone. The town's name, in fact is derived from the Saracen word "Kalat" meaning castle and the word "gerum" meaning grotto or cave. In 1030 the Genovese had possession of the city for a brief period to which certain Ligurian linguistic influences bear witness in the form of the local dialect. The cult of Saint George also suggests Ligurian influence in the area. In 1693 it was rebuilt on an even grander scale than before after its destruction by an earthquake. Caltagirone is considered to be the Faenza of Sicily because of the mass production of ceramics of which the most valuable are those pieces which date back to the 17th and 18th centuries. Although the patterns are often irregular or copied from other designs from other parts of Italy, they are extremely attractive because of their brilliant colours. A local gentleman, Gesualdo di Bartolo brought the beautiful Caltagirone ceramics to fame in modern times and his large collection is still on show in the town.

The 17th century Cathedral has a 19th century façade and inside you can see the nave and two aisles in the form of a Maltese cross. You can see paintings by the local artist Francesco Vaccaro (19th cent.) behind the lateral alter and in the Treasury you can see a collection of sacred hangings. The Casino dei Nobili decorated by Gagini is also of interest, as is the Town Hall with its beautiful façade by G.V. Nicastro (19th cent.). Other places of interest to the visitor are the Baron's Palace with its Baroque cornice by the artist Gagini, the church of San. Giacomo restored between 1694 and 1708 which has a nave and two aisles forming a Maltese cross shape and a portal which was designed, signed and dated 1585 by the artist A. Gagini himself. In the sacrestia which is reached by a door in the left aisle, there is a beautiful silver urn containing the relics of Saint Giacomo on which six scenes from the Saint's life are depicted in bas-relief by the artists Nibilio and Giuseppe Gagini completed at the end of the 16th century.

The church of Saint Domenic flaunts a lively Baroque façade looking onto a small square at the end of which there is another church, **the Church of San Salvatore** also with a Baroque façade. It has an octagonal plan and possesses a beautiful "Madonna and Child" by Gagini (1532) A long flight of steps decorated with ceramic tiling, leads away from the town hall square. During the annual festival of the 25th July, the steps are illuminated with coloured lighting and millions of country people come to celebrate wearing traditional costumes.

From the 142nd step looking out to the left the eye falls on the ruins of a castle set in a vast panorama. If you walk round the villa you will come to **the Church of St. Maria del Gesù** with a 15th century portal. Inside you can see a "Madonna and Child" by the artist A. Gagini at the third alter to the left as you come in.

The stairway

Gela

Gela is an industrial city which deals in the commerce of, among other things oil which is extracted by the oil company Anic. Its existence can be traced back to prehistoric times, but the city itself was colonised by peoples from Rhodes and Crete in the 7th cent. B.C. In the 5th cent. it was devastated by the Cartheginians and rebuilt in the 4th cent. B.C. Once more, it was destroyed in the 3rd cent. by the Mamertini. Frederick II christened it "Terranova" (New Land) which was officially substituted by its old name in 1928.

On Good Friday a picturesque representation of

Head-antefixes of Giunone

the crucifixion is performed to commemorate Christ's death. Where the ancient acropolis once stood the remains of the *Quartiere Timoleonte* from the 4th century B.C. was discovered on the site of older buildings. The ruins of a 5th cent. Doric temple and also, a 6th cent. temple to the goddess Athena lie in the *Parco della Rimembranza.* From this panoramic point visitors can enjoy a view of the Gela valley below. In the nearby *archaeological museum* which is divided into separate sections you can see a large se-

lection of interesting exhibits from prehistoric times to more recent finds. Among these is a terracotta horse from the 5th cent. B.C. there are also finds from sanctuaries like the little clay statue of Demetra and others showing Athena sitting down, which you can see in the second room. The third room has finds discovered outside the city and the Acropolis on show, while the fourth exhibits material found within the city boundaries of Upper Capo which dates from the 4th to

the 3rd centuries B.C. a long with epigraphic evidence. In the fifth section of the museum there is a collection of documentary evidence on shrines outside the city walls and also, 5th century urns and fragments from a Greek necropolis (burial ground). The seventh room is dedicated to the exhibition of material from sites around Gela. The eighth room shows finds from the Paleocristian and Medieval periods. An interesting private collection of Attic terracotta and earthenware is on show and in conclusion

there is also an interesting numismatic collection of Sicilian and Athenian coins. 4th century *Greek baths* show the system of baths and demonstrate techniques used to heat the water. A beautiful example of Neoclassical architecture can be seen in Piazza Umberto I in the 17th century church known as *Chiesa Matrice.*

Kamarina - Ragusa

Kamarina and its ruins are situated 19.6 km. from the road that leads to the Fattoria Pace di Piombo (Peace of Lead Farm). It was originally a Syracusan colony founded in 598 B.C. at the mouth of the Ippari river. It was destroyed by the Romans in 258 B.C. but some tracts of the original ancient city walls, the ruins of the canal-port, the foundations of a temple to the goddess Athena and a part of the Hellenistic-Roman urban quarter, have been preserved. They are the *casa dell'Altare* (House of the alter), *casa dell'Iscrizione* (House of the Inscription), *casa del Mercante* (House of the Merchant) and a part of the southern necropolis of *Passo Marinaro (Sailor's Walk)*. A small "*Antiquarium*" has been stored in the **Villa Pace** (House of Peace) while a museum which will eventually house all the finds that have already been excavated, is being prepared.

Ragusa is situated on the slopes of the Hyblaean Mountains between two vast concave valleys and is made up of two main centres, one is the Medieval Ragusa Ibla which is about 380 metres above sea level and the other more recent town centre which follows a regular chequered plan which is about 500 metres above sea level.

It was founded by the people of Dalmatian Ragusans in the 8th century on the old site of *Hybla Heraia*. A Byzantine castle was built here which was later conquered by Arab invaders in 848. Ruggero I of Altavilla made this city the headquarters of the county in 1091, which Manfredi Chiaramonte unified to Modica. Damaged by the 1542 earthquake and completely destroyed by 1693 earthquake, the city was rebuilt and divided into two municipalities in 1862, Upper Ragusa and Lower Ragusa.

The Old Church of Saint George

Ragusa Ibla boasts a grand *St. George's Basilica* at the top of a monumental flight of steps from where it dominates the whole town of Ibla. It was built between 1738 and 1775 on a plan thought by Rosaro Gagliardi and manifests the majesty of Baroque style in its façade which is divided into three parts by friezes, columns and elegant decorative motifs. Inside, there is a nave and two aisles where Renaissance sculptures are on show. There is also a Treasury.

The St. Joseph's Church is of the same stylistic importance as the Cathedral itself, and is also attributed to the work of Gagliardi. Inside there is a beautiful silver statue of St. Joseph from the 16th century.

In **the Ibleo Gardens**, which is a public park, you can see the *St. Dominic's Church* with its belfry decorated in ceramic tiling and the *The Church of the Old Cappuccini Monks* which holds paintings by Pietro Novelli. The *Old Church of Saint George* stands just outside the public gardens, and it has a magnificent 15th century portal in Catalan-Gothic style.

The Cathedral of Ragusa in Piazza S. Giovanni was built in the 18th century and has an elaborately decorated façade. The nave and two aisles inside are decorated with stuccowork as are the 18th century chapels, also inside the cathedral. Behind the cathedral, stands the *Baroque style rectory*. Note the balconied windows.

The Archaeological Museum of Ibleo in via Natatelli houses a collection of archaeological finds dating from the Neolithic period to the Bronze Age that come from digs carried out in the area surrounding Ragusa. There are also exhibits excavated at the Camarina Necropolis, which date back to the ancient Hellenistic and Roman Periods. **The Church of St. Mary of The Stairs** was rebuilt after a terrible earthquake in 1693 and has among some of its most interesting features a bas-relief representation in terracotta of *The Virgin's Journey* which dates back to the 16th century. There is a flight of 242 steps, known as *Le Scale* that lead from the base of the church and link Ibla with Ragusa.

St. Joseph's Church

St. George's Church

Noto is situated in a beautiful position on a hill, on the slopes of the Hyblaean Mountains. In ancient times it was named *Neetum* and was influenced both politically and economically by Syracuse. Originally an important Roman colony, it was taken over by the Byzantines and later by the Arabs until its decline and eventual destruction by the 1693 earthquake. G.B. Landolina drew up a new town plan from which the city was rebuilt nearer the coast. This was slightly modified by Angelo Italia from Licata who added a regular system of roads to the lower part of the town. These parallel roads are intersected by narrower roads which lead uphill, and in the upper part of the town, an area called Pianoalto (High Plateau) they narrow down still further to become lanes and stairways. The monumental buildings built with local golden stone are a typical feature of these streets with their spectacular architecture and monumental steps.

The Civic Museum is in Corso Vittorio Emanuele and houses exhibits that date back to the Prehistoric, Greek, Medieval and modern periods.

The Municipal Square is bordered by **The Town Hall** formerly Palazzo Ducezio, which was the work of Vincenzo Sinatra of the 18th cent. It is surrounded by a portico and shows a grand 18th century façade between two bell towers.

The main door is the work of the contemporary artist G.F. Pirrone (1982) decorated with bronze squares which depict episodes from the life of Saint Corrado. Inside there is a nave with two aisles and in a silver urn, the relics of Saint Corrado Confaloniere, patron saint of

the city are preserved.

The 18th century **Bishop's Palace** and the Neoclassical *Church of St. Salvatore* mark the boundaries of the square to the right of the church while to the left the 18th cent. *Palazzo S. Alfonso* and the adjacent *Palazzo Villadorata* are typical of Sicilian Baroque style.

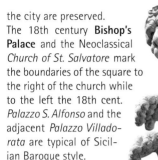

The Piazza XVI Maggio (16th May Square) is dominated by the Church of Saint Domenic which has a beautiful curvilinear façade and is flanked *to* the left by the *old Dominican Monastery* with its rusticated-ashler door.

The Municipal Library is now situated here. On the right there is the Hercules House with its central fountain on which a 17th century statue of Hercules is mounted.

Via Cavour runs parallel to Corso Vittorio Emanuele and it too is lined with interesting buildings, churches and convents from the 18th century. In the middle of *Pianalto*, the 18th century church Chiesa del Crocifisso stands. Two Romanesque lions guard the church on either side of the main door and inside you can see the magnificent statue of the *"Madonna of the Snow"* sculpted by Francesco Laurana in 1471. The ancient site of Old Noto lies 16 km to the north-east of the modern town. There you can visit the ruins caused by the earthquake in 1693 and still make out the remains of *the castle*, of the *Royal Gate* and of *the Hermitage of Divine Providence*.

The square

Sculpture of support for the balcony

The Cathedral

The restoration

The Infiorata

Ducezio palace

Noto Marina, a beautiful seaside resort, lies 8km. south east of the town centre and stretches down as far as the mouth of the Tellaro river.

The Greek city of Eloro with its 5th cent. fortifications once stood here.

The ancient theatre, a shrine to Demetra and the 10 metre high Pizzuta column made up of uncemented stone masses can also be seen.

The remains of a 4th cent. A.D. Roman Villa can be found at Caddeddi, not far from Eloro, in which you can admire the mosaic floors showing hunting scenes and a picture from the myth of Hector.

Syracuse is situated on the south-east coast of the island of Sicily on the small Isle of Ortigia which is joined to the mainland by a bridge. It is a very popular with tourists because of its interesting historical past to which the numerous ruins bear witness, its natural beauty and its wealth of classical architecture and history. It was founded in 734 B.C. as a Corinthian colony under the command of Archia and was an important commercial and political centre because of its strategic coastal position. Prosperity enabled the town to grow extending its boundaries inland to establish other colonies such as Acre, Enna, Casmene and Camerina. In the 5th century B.C. it fell into the hands of Gelone, Tyrrant of Gela who made it the capital city of his realm. Under his command and later, that of his brother Gerone the city thrived and prospered. Gelone subdued a revolt by the people of Camarina and together with Terone, Tyrrant of Agrigento, he defeated the Cartheginians at Imera in 480. His brother Gerone was an equally successful conqueror, fighting and defeating the Etruscans and Catania in a fierce battle at Enna in 474. Syracuse became such a successful port of trade and commerce that it attracted the attention of its main rival Athens which at that time was engaged in fighting the Peloponnesian Wars. Nevertheless, afraid of Syracuse's wealth and power, Athens made a disastrous attempt to stem the growth of the city by sending a contingent of soldiers to Sicily under the command of Alcibiades and Nicaea The city was also threatened by the Cartheginians who managed to capture Selinunte, Imera and Agrigento and attempted to colonize Syracuse. However, the Cartheginians were no match for Syracuse, led by Dionysius (406 - 397) who drove them out and in so doing restored the city to peace and prosperity. Dionysius was succeeded by his son Dionysius V and later Dion after which time the city began a slow decline which lasted up until the dictatorship of Agatocles who between 317 and 289 B.C. restored prosperity to the city. Aatocles also found himself battling against the old enemy Carthage. Under the rule of Gerone II, Syracuse went to war with the Mamertini, Rome's allies. Gerone wisely decided to ally himself with Rome so avoiding any involvement in the 1st Punic War. The city was home to many famous historical figures like the great poet Theocritus and the scientist Archemedes.

Under the leadership of Geronimo, Syracuse allied itself to Carthage against the Roman Empire. It was besieged by Claudius Marcellus who smashed through the vane defence lines with his war machines thought by Archemedes. The city was taken, sacked and left to a slow decline which reached its lowest ebb in Medieval times. It was occupied by the Arabs in the 9th century, by the Normans in the 11th century and by the Aragonese in the 14th century. The city only began to recover after it was rebuilt following the 1693 earthquake and once more began to flourish in the 17th and 18th centuries.

The Cathedral

The island of Ortigia is connected to the mainland by the *Ponte Nuovo* which leads to *Piazza Pancali* where you can see the ruins of the *Temple of Apollo*, the oldest Doric temple in Sicily dating back to the 6th century B.C. You can still see the foundations on which two trabeated columns stand. There are also the stumps of other columns and a part of the cell wall.

Maniace Castle

Castello Maniace is an example of military art. It was built by Frederick II of Swabia in 1230 and owes its name to the British General George Maniace who conquered Syracuse in 1038. It has a square shaped structure with cylindrical towers at each corner and a Gothic doorway.

The island of Ortigia

Both Virgil and Pindaro praised **the Fountain of Aretusa** in their writings. This unusual fountain contains saltish water probably caused by the infiltration of seawater into the fresh water spring. However, according to myth Aretusa, Artemis' companion, once went to bathe in the river Alfeo after the hunt. The river, captivated by the beauty of the nymph, fell in love with her and changed into human form so that he could follow her. The nymph ran to Artemis for help and he turned her into a water spring which he buried deep underground allowing her to resurface on the Island of Ortigia. In the meantime, Alfeo who had resumed the form of a river chased after her across the sea and when he reached her their waters were mixed together producing a saltish water fountain. The mythological river Alfeo is thought to be a spring known as the The Eye of Zillica. The myth is recorded on Syracusan coinage from the 5th to the 3rd centuries B.C. The coins were minted with a picture of the nymph shown with dolphins swimming about in her wavy hair.

Aretusa Spring

Cathedral Square is a magnificent expression of Baroque style. Surrounded by buildings of great architectural taste, it is dominated by the Cathedral, the *Palazzo Senatorio* (now the town hall headquarters) which was built by Giovanni Vermexio (1629 - 1633), the Palazzo Beneventano del Bosco, which was restructured in the 18th cent. and the *Archbishops Palace* also built by Andrea Vermexio in 1618. Note, also the *Church of Saint Lucia* with its 18th cent. façade.

Although **the Cathedral** has undergone numerous architectural improvements and renovations its style which is decidedly Baroque can be clearly seen in its impressive façade. It was built by Andrea Palma (1728 - 1754). However the main building of the church was originally a 5th century **Temple to Athena**, the beautiful Greek goddess. It was transformed in the 7th century into a Christian church with a nave and two aisles, by filling in the spaces between the original columns and turning the Greek cell into the central nave. Inside, visitors can feast their eyes on the wealth of art from the 12th cent. baptismal font mounted on four bronze lions, a laminated antependium in silver dating back to the 18th cent., which can be found in the second chapel on the south side to a Baroque statue of Saint Lucia lying on a sarcophagus in bas-relief. Note also *the Chapel of the Sacred Sacrament* built in 1653 which has a beautiful wrought iron gate, the *Chapel of the Crucifix* a Baroque alter and various sculptures of which there is a 16th cent. *"Madonna of the Snow"* and one of Saint Lucia by Antonello Gagini.

The Cathedral

Archemedes Square

Archemedes Square is surrounded by beautiful buildings like the Palazzo della Banca d'Italia with its magnificent courtyard and 4th century stairway. The 15th century Palazzo Lanza has magnificent mullioned windows with two lights. The *Fontana di Archemede* (Archemedes' Fountain), a piece of modern art-work has pride of place in the middle of the square. It shows the nymph Aretusa at the point of turning into a spring. Note the *Palazzo Montalto* in the road which bears its name, with its Gothic façade and magnificent mullioned windows with two and three lights.

The picturesque **Medieval part of the city** lies east of Piazza Archemedes. You can follow Via Maestranza lined with 15th century buildings until you reach the Baroque *St. Francis' Church* and then turn left into via Vittorio Veneto (formerly called Maestranza) which is the main high street of the Spanish part of Syracuse. Here you can see the Spanish influence in the architecture with their typical Spanish corbels.
The 15th century *Chiesa di S. Filippo* Neri (Saint Philip Neri) and the *Palazzo Interlandi* stand here and in Via   Mirabella you can admire the Palazzo Bongiovanni and the *Chiesa del Carmine* both dating back to the 17th century. You can also see the 15th century Palazzo Abela and the 12th century *Church of St. Thomas*. The Auditorium now occupies the *St. Peter's Church* which underwent many restorations and renovations and stands apart in a small niche.

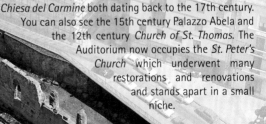

The Temple of Apollo

Palazzo Bellomo of Swabian origin (13th cent.) was restored in the 15th cent. is now occupied by the **Regional Art Gallery** which includes paintings and works of art from Medieval to modern times. Among the more famous sculptures on display on the first floor, you can see the *Madonna del Cardillo* by Domenico Gagini, the tomb stone of Giovanni Savastida by Francesco Laurana and the *sepulchre of Giovanni Cardinas* by Antonello Gagini (1506).

The paintings are on the first floor among which a triptych from the Russian School by Sraganov from the 16th century, Caravaggio's *"Saint Lucia's Burial"* (1609), a 14th century *"Saint Leonard"* attributed to Lorenzo Veneziano, a *"Madonna seated on the throne and Child"* by Pedro Serra from the 14th century and the tableau by Antonello da Messina showing the *"Annunciation"* (1474). There are several rooms dedicated to the display of jewellery, material, ceramics, embroidered fabrics and Sicilian furniture.

The Greek City: Syracuse covered a larger area in ancient times than today and includes Acradina, *Neapolis* and *Ziche* apart from the *Island of Ortigia*.

A long the edge of the north side of this part of the city there were once the Latomie or mines where whitish limestone was extracted to make monuments at Syracuse.

Over the years the rock was eroded and created steep gullies which today have been turned into gardens.

From via Paolo Orsi you can follow a long an ancient Roman road until you reach **the Archaeological Park of Neapolis.** Some tracts of the original road can still be seen on the corner of Viale Cavallari.

This area best represents the Greek city of Syracuse and includes **Gerone II's alter**, the Roman amphitheatre, the Greek theatre, the Latomie del Paradiso, dell'Intagliatella and S. Venere and also the Necropolis of Grotticelli.

You can get to the **Roman Amphitheatre** which was carved out of the rock by following a pathway lined with sarcophagi made of stone. It was built in the 3rd century A.D. and is only slightly smaller in size to the amphitheatre in Verona. The rectangular water cistern used to collect and store water for the amphitheatre is visible under the Chapel of Saint Nicholas.

The Greek Theatre is one of the grandest monuments that has come down to us from ancient times. It has a diameter of 140 metres and was built in the 5th century B.C. It was renovated several times by Gerone II in the 3rd century A.D. and later in Roman times (4th century A.D.). It has a cavea or seating gallery which is carved into the rock and divided into 9 sections or cunei. Out of the 61 original steps 46 have survived. Half way up the terrace there is a wide corridor (diazoma) which interrupts the steps and finishes in a stone slab where the names of all the gods and the members of Gerone II's family are inscribed. The different sections of the cavea or seating gallery were also named after members of the Tyrrant's family. The semicircular stalls which form the orchestra pit reaches as far as the foot of the terraced gallery. On the opposite side the few remnants of what was once the stage can be discerned.

The Latomia del Paradiso is a limestone mine which goes down 20 to 30 metres into the earth and includes the **Orecchio di Dionisio** (Dionysius' Ear) and the Grotto dei Cordari (The Cave of the Cordmakers).

Lerone II's alter forms a rectangle measuring 22.8 x 198 metres and is the largest Greek alter of this period.
It was built by the Tyrrant Gerone II in the 3rd century for public sacrifices though, only the base of it cut out of the rock remains to be seen.

The Greek Theatre

The Ropemakers Grotto was used by ropemakers for centuries. The play on light inside this cave is fascinating as is the colour of the rock and vegetation.

It is linked to the *Latomia del Paradiso* by a recently built tunnel which in turn links it to the *Latomia Intagliatella* with its high central horst citrus fruit trees.

An arch in the rock connects it to the *Latomia di Santa Venera* which has been transformed into a beautiful park.

The Grotticelli Necropolis can be reached by following a narrow path where there are numerous Greek tombs from Hellenistic, Roman and Byzantine periods. Among these is a dovecote called the Tomb of Archemedes with a Doric frontispiece and two lateral half columns.

The Cave of The Ropemakers

Dionysius' Ear is a 65 metre long tunnel 23 metres high and varying in width from 5 to 11 metres. It was given its present name by Caravaggio because of its shape and also its capacity to amplify sound. The legend of Dionysius recounts that Dionisyus used these caves to hear what his prisoners, which he kept there, said to each other.

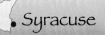

The Greek Theatre

The St. John's Catacomb under the church of S. Giovanni which was destroyed by the earthquake of 1693, can be reached by going down into the Crypt of San Marciano which has the shape of a Greek cross and is decorated with frescoes from different periods. In the catacomb there is an underground necropolis dating back to the 4th or 5th centuries where you can see millions of burial niches distributed a long the main gallery and also secondary galleries.

Villa Landolina with its garden planted with trees is the site of the Regional Archaeological Museum which houses a small Latomia which is the Protestant Cemetery. Here the German poet August von Platen was buried after his death at Syracuse in 1835.

The Regional Archaeological Museum planned by Franco Minissi and named Paolo Orsi after one of the archaeologists who contributed most significantly to the research and exploration of Sicilian territory, especially Syracuse. It is one of the most important archaeological museums in Italy housing objects left by prehistoric and protostoric civilizations in the Sicilian area. It also contains collections of Greek and Roman finds. The museum is well equipped with didactic aids in order to show the exhibits in their historical, social and environmental contexts. There are captions, dioramas, plans and maps and aerial photographs which give information about each item shown. The building extends horizontally in a kind of daisy pattern. In the centre the main meeting point provides visitors with general information about the various sections of the museum. For example the first section deals with geology, palaeontology and the prehistoric period of Sicily. Here you will find the remains of hippopotami and dwarf elephants. The second section is dedicated to finds excavated from the Ionic and Doric-Greek colonies, in particular from Megara, Hyblaea and Syracuse. The third section examines the so called sub-colonies of Syracuse. Another section deals with the Hellenistic-Greek and Roman periods.

The Latomia dei Cappuccini are fascinating for their size, irregular structure and rich vegetation. In 414B.C. 7,000 Athenian prisoners from Nicea's army were held here after being defeated by the Syracusans.

The Sepulchre of Santa Lucia was built in piazza Santa Lucia where the saint was martyred. It is of Byzantine origin but was restructured by the Normans in the 12th century and altered in the 1600s. The famous "Seppellimento di Santa Lucia" (Saint Lucia's Burial) by Caravaggio was once kept in the apse but is now at Palazzo Bellomo.

The octagonal Chapel called **The Chapel of the Sepulchre** built by Giovanni Vermezio in the 17th century contains the burial niche where the Saint Lucia was to be buried. Her body was sent to Constantinople by George Maniace and then brought back to Venice by the Crusaders in 1204

and deposited in the Church of Saint Geremia where it remains to this day. The catacombs of Saint Lucia are among the most complex in Italy having a central part that goes back to the 3rd century and galleries that run beneath the church and Piazza Santa Lucia.

Piazza della Vittoria reveals traces of an old 5th century road which led to the amphitheatre and a shrine dedicated to Demetra and Kore. The road was discovered because of the numerous devotional statuettes found on the site. Behind the piazza stands the *The Sanctuary dedicated to the Madonna of Tears* built to preserve a bolster with the effigy of the Madonna on it. This effigy was seen weeping in 1953 by a family of modest means in their house. The bolster was transferred to the Sanctuary and housed in a modern building built in 1955.

Foro Siracusano is now a square in the middle of a modern part of the city where a monument dedicated to those who died in the War now stands. It was originally, however the agora di Acradina (assembly place), the most important area of Greek Syracuse.

The Roman Gymnasium is a monumental Roman building which dates back to the 1st cent. A.D. with an arcaded court, a temple and a theatre. Many statues have been found here with inscriptions dedicated to Serapis which have led experts to believe that there was temple dedicated to eastern cults here. Because this area is actually below sea level it is subject to frequent flooding.

Temple of Giove Olimpo

Castello Eurialo is the most ingenious military building that was constructed by the Greek civilization. It stands on the highest part of the Epipoli plain.

It was altered in the Byzantine period as a defence against the threat of an Arab invasion. Three deep ditches were dug and vertical walls were carved of of the rock with a system of underground galleries and passage ways to allow the troops to move quickly from one place to another.

Castle Eurialo

Catania lies in the middle of the east coast of the island in beautiful surroundings at the foot of Mount Etna. It lies at the furthest northern point from the valley that bears the same name. It has the second highest population and has a healthy economy. The first evidence of the origins of Catania have been traced back to prehistoric times with the discovery of a settlement of Calcidese from Catinon. It was conquered by Gerone of Syracuse who named it Aetna but was restored to its founders again in 461 B.C. who changed its name back to what it had been before. In the second half of the 3rd century B.C. the Romans transformed the city into a colony in which state it enjoyed a long period of peace and tranquillity. In the 6th century, however, it fell into the hands of the Ostrogoths, then the Byzantines and later the Arabs. In the 11th century the Normans took over and it is to them that the building of the Cathedral is attributed. The city went on to be subjected to Swabian rule which in turn gave way to the Aragonese invasion. The Aragonese were responsible for the construction of the Ursino Castle. When Etna erupted in 1669 the city was covered in a thick layer of lava which covered a distance of 2 km.

Yet another natural disaster struck in 1693 when a terrible earthquake claimed the lives of almost a third of the city's' inhabitants. G.B. Vaccarini was responsible for rebuilding the city from a plan designed by the Duke of Camastra which gave the city its distinctive Baroque style. The city participated in the Risorgimento in the 19th century and upheld Garibaldi's beliefs. During the Second World War it was badly damaged by bombs and has since become the modern town of Catania that we see today. It is a great tourist attraction often chosen as a holiday destination for its vicinity to the coast and to the volcano Etna and also for the opportunity to do sport and go on excursions that it offers. It is also an important commercial and industrial centre having a very active port second only to the port of the capital city of Palermo. A good time of year to visit Catania is in February when a colourful festival is held in honour of the patron saint of the city, Saint Agatha. The festival lasts for three days, from 3rd to 5th February. On the 3rd there is a parade of the "Cannalore" which are 6m. long wooden poles painted in gold and engraved with the symbols of all the old city guilds.

Piazza del Duomo (Cathedral Square) lies at the heart of the city and offers a varied and lively architectural prospect of the Dome, St. Agatha Abbey, the Town Hall, the old Clerical seminary and the **Fontana dell'Elefante** (The Elephant Fountain) by Vaccarini in the centre. An Egyptian obelisk stands on top of an elephant made of volcanic stone which in turn stands on a marble base, probably dating back to Roman times. It has become the symbol of the city and is known locally as the "Liotru". **The Cathedral** was built in 1092 and rebuilt by G. Palazzotto in 1693, after it was destroyed by an earthquake in 1169. However, reconstruction work was not completed until 1758 when G.B. Vaccarini took over from Palazzotto. Apart from the Chapel of St. Agatha, there are other sights of great interest, among which the monument to Bellini, the Renaissance marble door and the Baroque bell tower must be mentioned. **St. Agatha's Church** in via Vittorio Emanuele II was originally the monastery of Saint Agatha but now shows the distinctive Baroque style of Vaccarini's architectonic plan. It was consecrated to Saint Agatha by Ferdinand IV and Pio VI in 1735 and must be considered as one of the most beautiful examples of 18th century Sicilian architecture built of limestone with a majestic stairway leading up to it.

The Collegiate Church in via Etnea, which is known as "the sitting-room of Catania", and was built by the Aragonese. The architect A. Amato was responsible for its construction following a plan drawn up by A. Italia in 1700 and completed by Stefano Ittar. Its name "Collegiata" refers to the times when it was used by a collegiate of priests. **The Chiesa di S. Benedetto** (St. Benedict's Church) designed by Alonzo di Benedetto (1704 to 1713) is the first of a series of 18th century churches in Via dei Crociferi and its magnificent prospect shows the influence of the architect Vaccarini. **The Chiesa dei Gesuiti** (Church of the Jesuits) was designed by Angelo Italia at the end of the 18th century. Inside the cupola visitors can admire frescoes that depict "l'esaltazione della compagnia di Gesù" (The Exaltation of Jesus' Disciples)by O. Sozzi. Once a boarding school, today it is an Art Institute.

The Chiesa di S. Giuliano (St. Julian's Church) also in via dei Crociferi is the most important building of the group and was the work of G.B. Vaccarini in 1760. It has a large alter which is heavily decorated with marble and rare bronzes and which bears an ornate Byzantine cross at its centre.

Cathedral Square

Palestro square

Ursino Castle

The harbour

St. Nicholas' Church

The Chiesa di S. Nicolò (St. Nicholas' Church) in Piazza Dante still shows an unfinished façade but is the largest church in Sicily. Inside visitors can see a sun-dial completed in 1841 in the south transept and unusual engravings on the floor of the signs of the zodiac, apart from the 17th and 18th century frescoes and canvasses. In the presbytery visitors can see a magnificent wooden choir dating back to the 1700s. There is also a grand organ made by the Neapolitan Donato del Piano (1755 - 1767) with 5 key boards, 72 registers and 2,916 organ pipes. The left transept leads to the Cappella dei Caduti (Chapel to the Fallen Soldiers) where the bodies of Catanese who died in the First World War are buried. Note the Rococò sacrestia. From the cupola you can enjoy a magnificent view over the whole city.

The Odeon in via Teatro Greco is a small semicircular theatre which was used in the Roman period for rehearsals that were then performed in the Amphitheatre.

The **Greek Theatre** in via Teatro Greco was most certainly built in the Roman period on the site of an ancient Greek theatre from the 5th century B.C. of which the only remaining parts are the vaulted ambulatory, the central nucleus of the seating gallery or cavea and part of the orchestra pit with its marble paving. It measured 86m. in diameter and had a seating capacity for 7.000 spectators.

The Achilleane thermal baths

The **Amphitheatre in Piazza Stesichoro** was also built in the Roman period in the 2nd century and was able to hold 15.000 spectators.

It was only slightly smaller in size than the Colosseum in Rome. The foundations stretch under the modern buildings of the city and it is the largest arena of all the known Roman theatres in Italy.

To the north of piazza Stesichorus stands Villa Bellini with its beautiful urban park full of palm trees and marvellous orangeries.

The **Teatro Massimo Bellini** which stands in a square named after it is a San-sovino inspiration. The façade is abundantly covered with bas-relief decorations. Inside there is a gorgeous hall on four tiers with a gallery at the top of very refined taste. Its inauguration took place with the "Norma" on 31 May 1890.

Etna is the largest active volcano in Europe and dominates one whole side of Sicily with its impressive mass. It's 3,350 m. high and has a perimeter of 165 km. and a surface area of 1,300 sq. km. Etna is considered to be quite a young volcano having been active for a relatively short period of 500,000 years. It is made up of various parts, **Trifoglietto** where over the centuries the **Valle del Bove** has been formed in the 5km. wide depression with its steep walls. The part known as **Mongibello** is almost continually active. There are four active craters in the main cone, the **Central crater**, the **Bocca Nova** (New Mouth) active since 1968, the **North-East Crater** and the **South-East underground Crater**. Lateral eruptions have given the slopes of Etna a corrugated appearance interrupted by numerous cracks and craters. Among the numerous eruptions that have taken place over the centuries, and at least 135 episodes have been recorded since the beginning of history, the most famous and tragic of all was the eruption of 1669 that lasted 122 days and was preannounced by three days of earthquakes. The volcanic deposits spewed out by the volcano has formed various hills like the Red Mountains which changed the shape of the volcano causing a torrent of lava to flow as far as Catania destroying part of the city and pouring into the sea for a distance of half a kilometre. Some of the slopes of the volcano are cultivated and citrus fruit trees, orchards and vineyards can be seen growing on the slopes below 1,100 metres. Part of the slopes have been given over to the cultivation of chestnut forests, holm-oaks and wonderful expanses of broom and oaks below 1,500 metres. From this height to 1,900 metres an area of beech trees and birch trees stretches up the slopes. At about 2,000 metres an evocative wild expanse of land rolls up the mountain side and for half the year is covered with snow. In winter visitors can use

the ski plants equipped with a network of ski-lifts which take you up at different points of the mountain side. The Regione Sicilia passed a law in May 1981 declaring the opening of the **Natural Park of Etna** in order to protect the natural beauty and singularity of the area. You can visit this zone by choosing from a varied itinerary of walks and treks, of which the most popular are the following: **the tour of Etna** which proposes a panoramic road of about 140 km. which goes right round the mountain passing Catania, Acireale, Giare, Fiumefreddo, Linguaglossa, Randazzo, Adrano, Paternò. Following this road the visitor will notice the varied countryside which changes from lush greenery to desolated expanses of lava. There are also points of historical and artistic interest to be seen on the way. The second most popular itinerary is the **Climb up to the Crater** which proposes two different routes by which tourists can reach the top of the crater. One road approaches the crater from the south side and the other from the north side. The south side route is about 35 km. long and leads up to the mountain refuge known as the Rifugio Sapienza at about 1,910 km. passing through Gravina di Catania, Mascalucia and Nicolosi on the way. Visitors can reach the refuge by cablecar which goes up to a height of 700 metres. From this point special means of transport are provided to tackle the rough road that leads to **The Philosopher's Tower** and the central crater a long a spectacular scenic route. The scenery around the crater is unique in its breathtaking beauty. The northern approach road passes through Linguaglossa and ends at **Piano Provenzana** at 1,810 km. Special transport is provided to take visitors from this point up the sides of the mountain. Travelling through what looks very much like a lunar landscape the road brings visitors out at **Piano delle Concazze** at a height of 3,000 metres from which point a guide escorts visitors to the central crater.

According to the legend which Ovid wrote about in the' Metamorphoses', the Cyclops, Polyphemus fell madly in love with the nymph Galatea who, herself was in love with the shepherd Aci, son of Fauno. One night the Cyclops surprised the two lovers together and became so angry that he threw a great mass of lava at Aci, killing him in the process. Galatea wept so much at the loss of her lover, that the god of the sea Neptune was moved to pity and so, to placate her, he transformed Aci's blood into a stream so that he could rejoin his beloved Galatea. This is the reason why so many of the place names begin with the word "Aci", for example Acicastello, Acitrezza, Acireale, Aci S. Antonio, Aci S. Lucia, Aci Catena and Acireale where there is a street that bears the name "Galatea" and in the public gardens del Belvedere there are the marble statues of Galatea crying over the body of Aci. **Acireale** is an ancient city which has now become a tourist resort and a popular spa. It is situated on a flat lava plain overlooking the sea. It is a common destination with tourists who come to see the wealth of art that this city is home to and to enjoy the mild climate. The Cathedral and the Palazzo Comunale (Town Hall) are among the places to see here.

Acicastello is a seaside town of Medieval origin. It is, today a very popular seaside resort. The Norman Castle built of black lava in about 1,000 is of particular interest. It was destroyed by Frederick II of Aragon in 1297. **Acitrezza** is in the same county which has a beautiful beach the Lido dei Ciclopi (Lido of the Cyclops) but its real claim to fame is that it served as a background setting for Giovanni Verga's novel "I Malavoglia" which is one of the finest works in 19th century Italian literature. In the main square there is a high relief representing some women waiting on the beach for their menfolk to return from fishing in stormy seas. The scene is summed up by a phrase written by Verga "E quei poveretti sembravano tante anime del purgatorio" ("And those poor women seemed like so many souls in Purgatory"). Today that once poor suburb is now a much frequented seaside town. The **Isola dei Ciclopi** are picturesque basalt rocks called "Faraglioni" that stick up out of the Acitrezza sea. The largest of these islands is **Isola di Lachea** which was given to the University of Catania by the Marquis Gravina to promote the biological and physical research of the sea around these coasts. In the IX Canto of Homer's **Odyssey** the writer narrates that these land masses were thrown at Ulysses and his companions by the blinded Polyphemus, as they tried to escape.

Acicastello

Acitrezza by night - Cliffs

Acireale

Giarre

Giarre is a lively little town with a marvellous Cathedral at its heart, which was built by P. Valente.

Joined to the small village of Riposto, Garre extends out towards Etna. It is a beautiful land full of lush orchards, vineyards and citrus fruit gardens crossed by winding roads that lead upwards to the highest parts of the volcano. The numerous streams of black lava that have overflowed down these slopes is a constant reminder of centuries of eruptions.

The gorges of Alcantara

The gorges of Alcantara

Gole dell'Alcantara is situated on the main eastern Sicilian high road number 114 that leads to Catania and Taormina by-passing The Naxos Gardens and going on to Francavilla di Sicilia (main road number 185). About 12 km. further on the road leads to Gole dell'Alcantara which is a magnificent recess cut into the lava by the river. The gole or gorges are only a few metres wide but are over 20 metres deep having steep vertical sides. The landscape here is wild and arid showing an unusual basalt columns which form evocative prismatic shapes which were formed by the stream of basaltic lava devoid of silicon but rich in iron, magnesium and calcium which make it particularly fluid. As the lava gradually cooled down it contracted causing it to split into prismatic shapes, pentangular sections and hexagonal forms. These rather spectacular geometric shapes were uncovered and polished up by the corrosive action of the water flowing over the surface over a period of tens of millions of years. The river is a of a metallic colour that changes varying from various shades of the hard steel grey reflected off the rocks. The river flows quietly and gently in places and in others it winds into little rivulets and splashes down waterfalls changing its colour almost to suit its mood, be it quiet or boisterous and reflecting the colours and light of a surrounding countryside which at this point seems almost unearthly. The gorges are carved out of the slopes of Mount Etna and were formed by the overflow of moulten lava which oozed out of the Molo crater. Visitors can enjoy magnificent prospective views from the river banks and also from the high basalt walls of the gorge. There are certain places a long the course of the river where the water is only a few centimetres deep allowing visitors to walk a long the river bed and explore the recesses of the gorge which at close sight are even more impressive. Looking up from the river bed at the menacing rocks that tower above the river going upwards vertically and limiting the narrow, winding corridor whose vibrant surface seems almost like a piece of futuristic sculpture.

Giardini Naxos (Naxos Gardens)

The Giardini Naxos, or the Naxos Gardens near Taormina is a well known tourist spot. It boasts first class facilities for tourists and spacious beaches. Not far away, Capo Schisò created by streams of lava that flowed from a prehistoric crater known as Mount Mòjo is a place where many archaeological excavations have been carried out. The Mòjo is considered as the most "eccentric" crater on Etna and it marks the place, where, in 735 B.C. the Greeks landed and established the city of Naxos. Three centuries later, however, their first colony was devastated by the Syracusans. The 6th century B.C. **walls** still showing some of the original **city gates**, a **tower** and an area thought to have been the site of a **shrine** bear witness to this terrible seige. The ruins of a temple dedicated to **Aphrodite** which date back to the 7th and 5th centuries B.C. have been discovered here a long with an **alter** and two **kilns** perhaps once part of the sanctuary that stood here. Another area of this archaeological zone includes the ruins of a city that was rebuilt after its destruction in 476B.C. in which the remains of places of

worship, craftsmen's', potter's and sculptor's shops have been discovered. Visitors can see more of the finds which include ceramics, objects made of clay, sculptures, terracotta objects and fragments of architecture, in the **Archaeological Museum of Naxos** which is housed in the old Bourbonic Fort at Cape Schisò.

Panorama of Giardini Naxos and Taormina

Taormina is situated on the slopes of Mount Tauro at a height of about 200metres above sea level. It is the queen of the promontory which juts out into the Ionian Sea. It is an enchanting, quiet dream-town where a thousand terraces overlook the sea. It is both aristocratic and friendly, a town of smiles and monuments, a flourishing witness to eternal natural beauty. It is also a place that is steeped in history, the history of its glorious past, apart from being an elegant holiday destination where tourists can drink in the atmosphere coloured by a thousand flowers which crowd the quiet streets and the brilliantly coloured Sicilian puppets that enliven the bazaars all around. Taormina has a mild, maritime climate and is always warm and sunny. In fact the number of sunny days registered here every year is very high. It was founded by the Siculi in 358 B.C. and was later colonised by the Greeks who left a splendid 3rd century theatre here, the second largest in Sicily measuring 115 metres in diameter. It was later rebuilt by the Romans in the 2nd century A.D. and, is today used to as an art gallery and arts centre where classical plays and film festivals are held. From the platea, in part carved into the rock and divided into 9 sections or "cunei", and also, from the terraces above the stage visitors can enjoy a marvellous view of Mount Etna and Calabria. For many years the history of Tauromenion, as the Greeks called it, was inextricably linked to the history of Syracuse. After Syracuse lost its independence during the 2nd Punic War it allowed Taormina to become part of the Roman federation to which it had to pay extra taxes.

Panorama

In 36 B.C. Octavius destroyed the city dividing up the confiscated territory among the Roman colonials who had fought for Augustus.

After the fall of the Roman Empire it became the capital of Byzantine Sicily but was later destroyed by the Arabs in 902 by whom it was rebuilt. It then fell into the hands of Ruggero d'Altavilla in 1079 under whose command the town flourished. Trouble was not far away, when in 1282 during the Vespri Wars, Taormina which was loyal to Spain sided with the Aragonese against the French.

In 1674 the French succeeded in occupying the town which was punished for not having taken part in the Revolt of Messina. In 1943 it was badly bombarded during the allied lading in Sicily, however in the years before the 1st World War many foreigners, above all Englishmen and Germans bought houses here and built villas.

The city has also hosted distinguished guests, such as the Emperor William II. Edward VII, the King of Siam, the Rothschilds the Morgans and the Krupps. Visitors must make a point of seeing the **Cathedral** of S. Nicola built in the 13th century and renovated in the 18th century which resembles a Norman church with its austere façade and square shape.

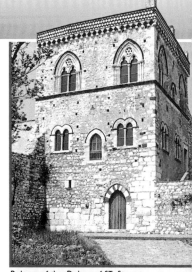

Palace of the Dukes of ST. Steven

Piazza IX Aprile (9th April Square)

A view of the Odeon

The Cathedral

The old College (4th century)

The Greek Theatre

Taormina

Corso Umberto is the main high street of the city and runs from **Porta Messina** to **Porta Catania** with **Piazza IX Aprile** half way between them. From the centre of the city you can see Etna. Several impressive buildings face onto the square, among which are, the Gothic **St. Augustin's Church**, the **Porta di Mezzo** with the **Clock Tower** above it. A long stairway leads from the Piazza Duomo to the 15th century **Palazzo Ciampoli**, behind which the **Badia Vecchia** which is the ruins of a 14th century palace with a merloned tower and tracery windows with two lights stands. Following Corso Umberto you eventually arrive at Porta Catania which is decorated on the outside with a niche showing the Aragonese coat of arms and also that of Taormina. Just before the gateway and a little to the left you can see **Palazzo dei Duchi di Santo Stefano** which is an elegant building decorated with tracery windows and a corona embellished with calcium and lava inlays dat-

Characteristic view

ing back to the 14th and 15th centuries. **Piazzale San Domenico** is situated south of the Cathedral and bears the name of the Church of St. Dominique which was destroyed by bombs during the War in 1943. However, the 16th cent. bell tower can still be admired as can the old convent, now turned into a hotel. **Porta Messina** is situated near Piazza Vittorio Emanuele and brings us out of the city. From via Pirandello it leads to **Belvedere** which is a terrace on a cliff top that falls sheer to the sea below. From here visitors have a marvellous view of the coast. **Palazzo Corvaia**, a severe 15th cent. building dominates Piazza Vittorio Emanuele. The façade, decorated at the top with merlons shows tracery windows with two lights which are separated by thin columns and a portal or main door of a Catalan-Gothic style. A long the via Teatrino Romano, to one side of the Palazzo Corvaia, a small Roman theatre called the Odeon stands facing the square. It was built in the Roman imperialistic period. The cavea, or seating gallery is divided, laterally into 5 cunei or sections.

The Greek Theatre

Isola Bella (Beautiful Island)

Mazzarò Beach

INDEX

© Copyright 2010 by
Officina Grafica Bolognese S.r.l.
Via del Fonditore, 6/5 - 40138 Bologna - Italia
Tel. +39 051 532 203 - Fax +39 051 532 188
e-mail: info@ogbsrl.it - www.ogbsrl.it
All rights reserved. Any reproduction (even if only partial) is forbidden.
Printed in UE by Officina Grafica Bolognese S.r.l. - Bologna - Italy
Text: Prof. Teresa Sapienza
Pictures by: Archivio OGB, G. Guardo, A. Parisi, M. Santangelo, Fulvio
Printed in march 2010 - ISBN: 9788860780768